OCR

Biology AS

Student Workbook

Model Answers: 2012

This model answer book is a companion publication to provide answers for the exercises in the **OCR AS Biology Student Workbook** 2012 edition. These answers have been produced as a separate publication to keep the cost of the workbook itself to a minimum, as well as to prevent easy access to the answers by students. In most cases, simply the answer is given with no working or calculations described. A few, however, have been provided with more detail because of their difficult nature.

ISBN 978-1-877462-84-9

www.biozone.co.uk

Published by BIOZONE International Ltd

BIOZONE

Additional copies of this Model Answers book may be purchased directly from the publisher

UK & EUROPE:
BIOZONE Learning Media (UK) Ltd.
Bretby Business Park, Ashby Road, Bretby,
Burton upon Trent, DE15 0YZ, **UK**
Telephone: 01283-553-257
Fax: 01283-553-258
Email: sales@biozone.co.uk

AUSTRALIA:
BIOZONE Learning Media Australia
P.O. Box 2841, Burleigh BC,
QLD 4220, **Australia**
Telephone: +61 7-5535-4896
Fax: +61 7-5508-2432
Email: sales@biozone.com.au

REST OF WORLD:
BIOZONE International Ltd.
P.O. Box 13-034,
Hamilton 3251, **New Zealand**
Telephone: +64 7-856-8104
Fax: +64 7-856-9243
Email: sales@biozone.co.nz

Contents

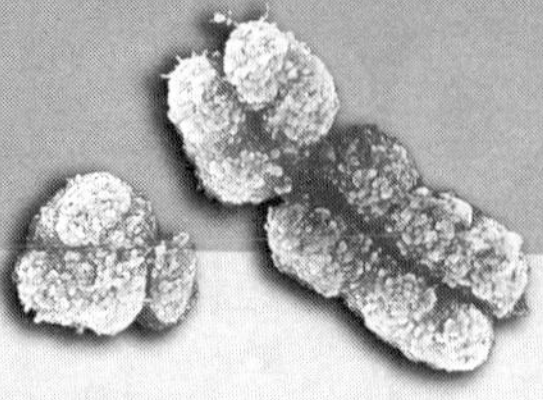

Contents

Contents

Hypotheses and Predictions (page 9)

1. Prediction: Woodlice are more likely to be found in moist habitats than in dry habitats.

2. (a) **Bacterial cultures**:
   Prediction: Bacterial strain A will grow more rapidly at 37°C than at room temperature (19°C).
   Outline of the investigation: Set up agar plates of bacterial strain A, using the streak plating method. Place 4 plates in a 37°C incubator and 4 on the lab bench. Leave all 8 plates for the same length of time (e.g. 24 hours), with all other conditions identical. Measure the coverage of the agar plates with bacteria (as a percentage).
   (b) **Plant cloning**:
   Prediction: A greater concentration of hormone A increases the rate of root growth in plant A.
   Outline of the investigation: Set up 6 agar plates infused with increasing concentrations of hormone A (e.g. 1 mgl^{-1}, 5 mgl^{-1}, 10 mgl^{-1}, 50 mgl^{-1}, 100 mgl^{-1}, 500 mgl^{-1}), and each plate with 12 clones of plant A. Measure root length each day for 20 days.

Accuracy and Precision (page 11)

1. Accuracy: the correctness of the measurement, or how close a measurement is to the true value.
   Precision: the repeatability of the measurements, how close the measured values are to each other.

2. Measurements that are both accurate and precise give data close to the true mean of the parameter or population being sampled.

3. The researcher may still be able to obtain precise data (measurements that are grouped closely together), but they will not be able to achieve accurate data. Because the temperature probe is incorrectly calibrated, it will give measurements that are either higher or lower than the actual temperature at which enzyme denaturation is occurring. Until the temperature probe is correctly calibrated, the researcher will not be able to obtain accurate data about the denaturation temperature for enzyme A.

A Qualitative Practical Task (page 12)

1. (a) All samples had to be heated for the same amount of time to ensure they all received the same treatment conditions for reaction.
   (b) Stirring ensures maximum contact of substrate and enzyme therefore maximising reaction.

2. As the bananas ripen, the starch is converted to simple sugars fructose and glucose.

3. (a) Fructose is a ketose sugar, but it is converted to glucose in the basic reagent and the aldehyde group gives a positive test.
   (b) You cannot tell from the test results if the banana ripening resulted in conversion of starch to glucose alone or to fructose (fruit sugar) and glucose (in fact it is converted to both).

A Quantitative Practical Task (page 13)

1. Aim: To investigate the effect of temperature on the rate of catalase activity.

2. Hypothesis: The rate of catalase activity is dependent on temperature.

3. (a) Independent variable: Temperature.
   (b) 10-60°C in uneven steps: 10°C, 20°C, 30°C, 60°C.
   (c) Unit: °C
   (d) Equipment: A means to maintain the test-tubes at the set temperatures, e.g. water baths. Equilibrate all reactants to the required temperatures in each case, before adding enzyme to the reaction tubes.

4. (a) Dependent variable: Height of oxygen bubbles.
   (b) Unit: mm
   (c) Equipment: Ruler; place vertically alongside the tube and read off the height (directly facing).

5. (a) Each temperature represents a treatment.
   (b) No. of tubes at each temperature = 2
   (c) Sample size: for each treatment = 2
   (d) Times the investigation repeated = 3

6. It would have been desirable to have had an extra tube with no enzyme to determine whether or not any oxygen was produced in the absence of enzyme.

7. Variables that might have been controlled (a-c):
   (a) Catalase from the same batch source and with the same storage history. Likewise for the H_2O_2. Storage and batch history can be determined.
   (b) Equipment of the same type and size (i.e. using test-tubes of the same dimensions, as well as volume). This could be checked before starting.
   (c) Same person doing the measurements of height each time. This should be decided beforehand.

   Note that some variables were controlled: The test-tube volume, and the volume of each reactant. Control of measurement error is probably the most important after these considerations.

8. Controlled variables should be monitored carefully to ensure that the only variable that changes between treatments (apart from the biological response) is the independent (manipulated) variable.

Recording Results (page 15)

1. See the results table at the top of the next page.

2. The table would be three times as big in the vertical dimension; the layout of the top of the table would be unchanged. The increased vertical height of the table would accommodate the different ranges of the independent variable (full light, as in question 1, but also half light, and low light. These ranges would have measured (quantified) values attached to them.

Variables and Data (page 16)

1. Measure wavelength (in nm) using a spectrophotometer; which measures light intensity as a function of the colour (wavelength) of light.

2. These data are semi-quantitative because an arbitrary numerical value has been assigned to a qualitative scale. The numbers are correct in a relative sense, but do not necessarily indicate the true quantitative values.

		Trial 1 / CO_2 conc. in ppm											Trial 2 / CO_2 conc. in ppm											Trial 3 / CO_2 conc. in ppm										
		Minutes											Minutes											Minutes										
	Set up no.	0	1	2	3	4	5	6	7	8	9	10	0	1	2	3	4	5	6	7	8	9	10	0	1	2	3	4	5	6	7	8	9	10
Full light conditions	1																																	
	2																																	
	3																																	

Manipulating Raw Data (page 17)

1. Basic transformations of raw data identify important features (e.g. trends) of the data.
   Data transformation can identify trends early on. Often these transformations can help a researcher to set the direction for subsequent experimental work.

2. (a) Percentage.
   (b) Allows you to compare the relative number of species at each habitat.

3.

Incidence of cyanogenic clover in different areas

Clover plant type	Frost free area		Frost prone area		Totals
	Number	%	Number	%	
Cyanogenic	120	76	22	15	142
Acyanogenic	38	24	120	85	158
Total	158	100	142	100	300

Constructing Tables (page 18)

1. (a)-(b) any two of the following (all for achieved):
   - Tables provide a systematic record of information.
   - Tables provide a way of condensing data.
   - Tables provide a summary of results.
   - Tables show trends and relationships in the data.

2. To identify trends in the data. To help decide the best method of graphing the data.

3. (a) Allows the data to be summarised so that trends or patterns can be identified more easily than by presenting raw data alone. It also aids the researcher in deciding the best way to graph the data to show the trend.
   (b) Allows the researcher to determine if the data is normally distributed or skewed. This will determine how the data will be further manipulated.

4. So that the control values are easily identified and compared with the values obtained for the treatments. This allows the researcher and readers to determine if the treatments are having any real effect.

Constructing Graphs (page 19)

1. Graphs visually show a trend or relationship in data using a minimum of space.

2. (a) Appropriate scale shows the trend in the data most clearly. For example, if the scale is too compressed then it is difficult to see the trend.
   (b) A floating or broken axis may be used when there is a large gap between zero and where the data begins. This allows for the data trends to be more easily visualised.

3. (a) The time intervals on the X-axis are evenly spaced even though the time increments at which the data were recorded are not.
   (b) If the graph were plotted correctly then the data points would be stretched out. When the line of best fit was applied the slope of the plotted data would be much flatter than the original.

Drawing Bar Graphs (page 20)

1. (a) Table as below:

Species	Site 1	Site 2
Ornate limpet	21	30
Radiate limpet	6	34
Limpet sp. A	38	-
Limpet sp. B	57	39
Limpet sp. C	-	2
Catseye	6	2
Topshell	2	4
Chiton	1	3

   (b) Bar graph: *See the next page of graph solutions.*

Drawing Histograms (page 21)

1. (a) Tally chart totals as below:

Weight group	Total
45-49.9	1
50-54.9	2
55-59.9	7 (given)
60-64.9	13
65-69.9	15
70-74.9	13
75-79.9	11
80-84.9	16
85-89.9	9
90-94.9	5
95-99.9	2
100-104.9	0
105-109.9	1

   (b) Histogram: *See the next page of graph solutions.*

Drawing bar graphs:

Average abundance of eight mollusc species at two sites along a rocky shore

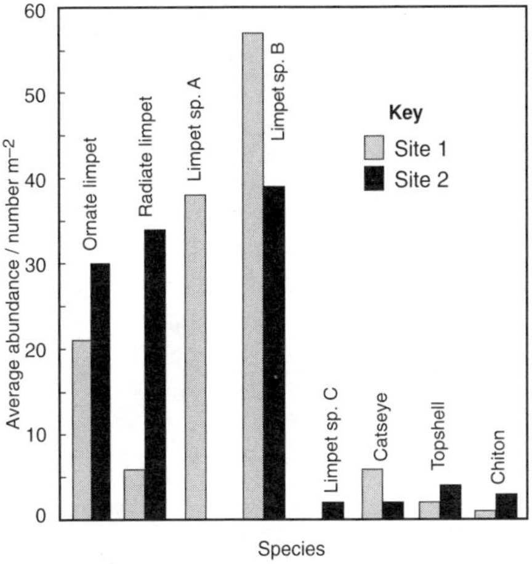

Drawing histograms:

Frequency histogram of weights of 95 individual males and females

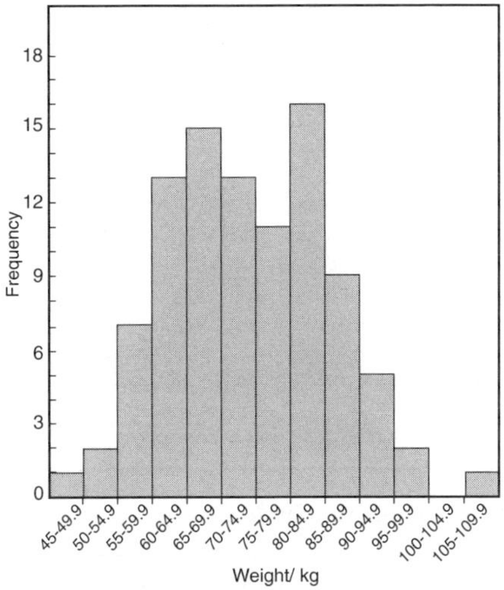

Drawing pie graphs:

Percentage occurrence of different food items in the diets of stoats, rats, and cats

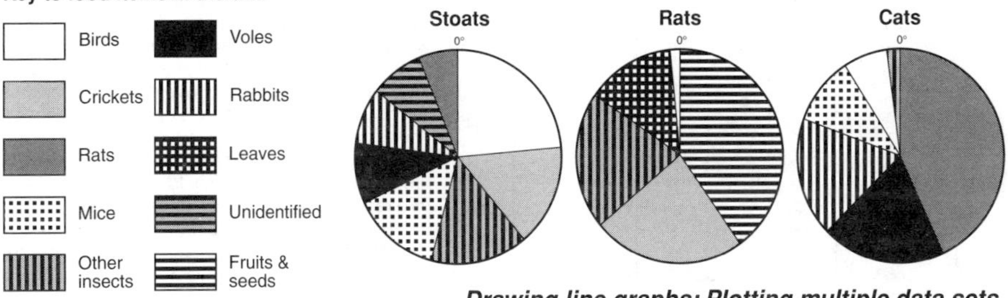

Drawing line graphs: Plotting multiple data sets

Numbers of deer and wolves on an island forest reserve between 1961 and 1969

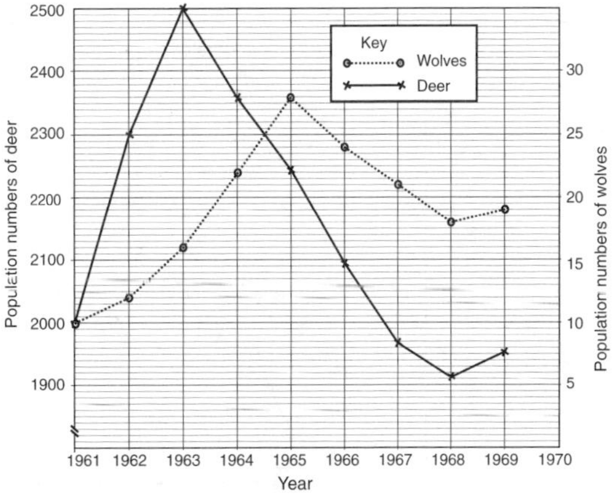

Drawing kite graphs:

Distribution of invertebrates along 3 different streams as indicated by biomass measured as wet weight/ g m^{-2}

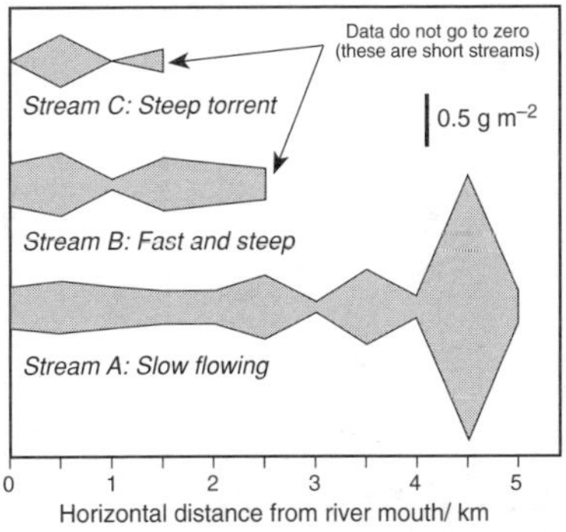

Drawing Pie Graphs (page 22)

1. (a) Tabulated data:

Food item in diet	Stoats		Rats		Cats	
	% in diet	Angle /°	% in diet	Angle /°	% in diet	Angle /°
Birds	23.6	85	1.4	5	6.9	25
Crickets	15.3	55	23.6	85	-	-
Insects	15.3	55	20.8	75	1.9	7
Voles	9.2	33	-	-	19.4	70
Rabbits	8.3	30	-	-	18.1	65
Rats	6.1	22	-	-	43.1	155
Mice	13.9	50	-	-	10.6	38
Fruits	-	-	40.3	145	-	-
Leaves	-	-	13.9	50	-	-
Unid.	8.3	30	-	-	-	-

(b) Pie graphs: *See previous page of graph solutions.*

Drawing Kite Graphs (page 23)

1. (a) Table:

Distance from mouth/ *km*	Wet weight/ *g* m^{-2}		
	Stm A	Stm B	Stm C
0	0.4	0.4	0
0.5	0.5	0.6	0.5
1.0	0.4	0.1	0
1.5	0.3	0.5	0.2
2.0	0.3	0.4	-
2.5	0.6	0.3	-
3.0	0.1	-	-
3.5	0.7	-	-
4.0	0.2	-	-
4.5	2.5	-	-
5.0	0.3	-	-

(b) Kite graph: *See previous page of graph solutions.*

Drawing Line Graphs (page 24)

1. (a) Line graph:

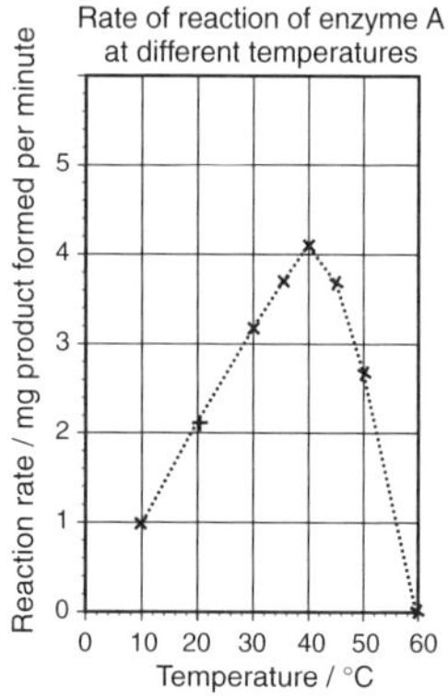

(b) Rate of reaction at 15°C = 1.6 mg product min^{-1}

2. (a) Line graph: See previous page of graph solutions.
   (b) The data suggest that the deer population is being controlled by the wolves. Deer numbers increase to a peak when wolf numbers are at their lowest; the deer population then declines (and continues declining) when wolf numbers increase and peak. **Teacher's note**: Control of the deer by the wolves is suggested, but not confirmed, by the data. In most natural systems, large predators do not control their prey, but are themselves controlled by the numbers of available prey, which are regulated by other factors such as food availability. In this case, the wolves were introduced to control deer and probably were. However, an equally valid interpretation of the data could be that the wolves are responding to changes in deer numbers (with the usual lag inherent in population responses), and the deer were already peaking in response to factors about which we have no information.

3. (a) Line graph and (b) point at which shags and nests were removed: See the graph below.

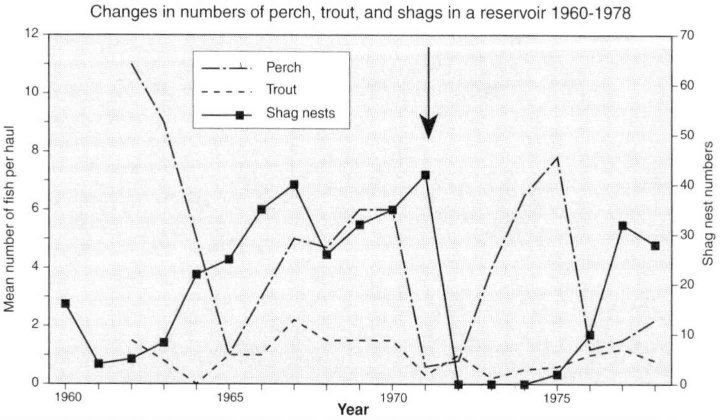

Interpreting Line & Scatter Graphs (page 27)

1. (b) **Slope**: Negative linear relationship, with constantly falling slope.
   Interpretation: Variable Y decreases steadily with increase in variable X.
   (c) **Slope**: Constant, level slope.
   Interpretation: Increase in variable X does not affect variable Y.
   (d) **Slope**: Slope rises and then becomes level.
   Interpretation: Variable Y initially increases with increase in variable X, then levels out (no further increase with increase in variable X).
   (e) **Slope**: Rises, peaks and then falls.
   Interpretation: Variable Y initially increases with increase in variable X, peaks and then declines with further increase in variable X.
   (f) **Slope**: Exponentially increasing slope.
   Interpretation: As variable X increases, variable Y increases exponentially.

2. (a) Perch fluctuations follow shag fluctuations closely.
   (b) The evidence suggests that the fluctuations of shag and trout numbers are not related, as trout numbers in 1967 peak before shag numbers.

Drawing Scatter Plots (page 28)

1. (a) Scatter plot and (b) Line of best fit:

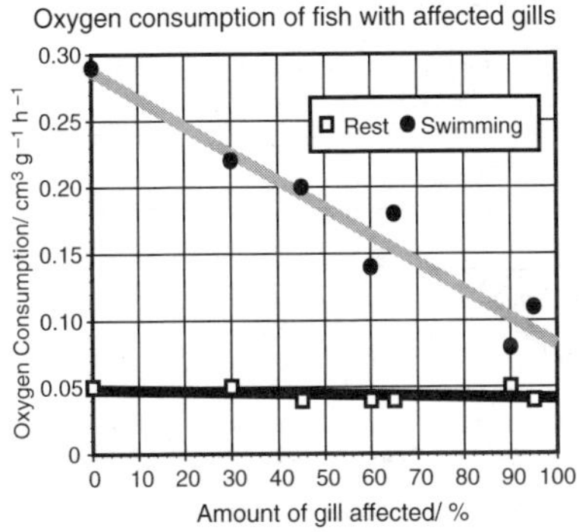

2. (a) At rest: No clear relationship; the line on the graph appears to have no significant slope (although this could be tested). **Note**: There is a slight tendency for oxygen consumption to fall as more of the gill becomes affected, but the scatter of points precludes making any conclusions about this.
   (b) Swimming: A negative linear relationship; the greater the proportion of affected gill, the lower the oxygen consumption.

3. The gill disease appears to have little or no effect on the oxygen uptake in resting fish.

Biological Drawings (page 29)

1. (a)-(h) any eight features in any order:
   - Lines cross over each other and are angled.
   - Cells are inaccurately drawn: they are not closed shapes, they do not even nearly represent what is actually there, there are overlaps.
   - There is no magnification given.
   - Drawing is cramped at the top corner of the page.
   - Labels are drawn on an angle.
   - There is no indication of whether the section is a cross section or longitudinal section.
   - There is a line to a cell type that has no label
   - Shading is inappropriate and does not indicate anything. It is apparently random and is unnecessary.
   - The material being drawn has not been identified accurately in the title by species.

2. Student's response required here. Some desirable features are shown in the figure below, but page position and size cannot be shown.

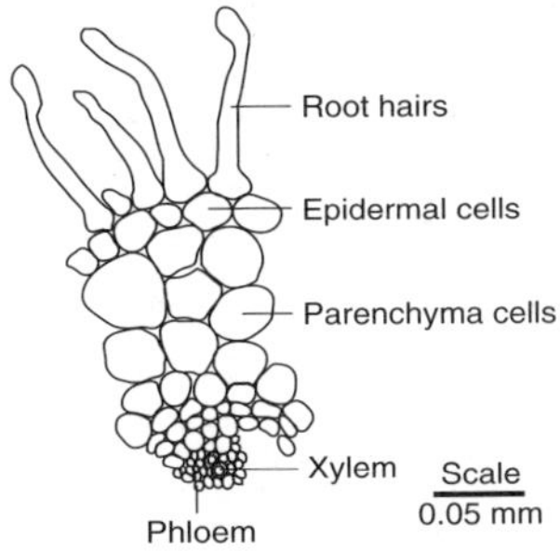

Root tranverse section from Ranunculus

3. A **biological drawing** is designed to convey useful information about the structure of an organism. From such diagrams another person should be able to clearly identify similar organisms and structures. By contrast, **artistic drawings** exhibit 'artistic licence' where the image is a single person's impression of what they saw. It may not be a reliable source of visual information about the structure of the organism.

Descriptive Statistics (page 31)

1. The modal value and associated ranked entries indicate that the variable being measured (sori per frond) has a bimodal distribution i.e. the data are not normally distributed. (Therefore) the mean and median are not accurate indicators of central tendency. Note also that the median differs from the mean; also an indication of a skewed (non-normal) distribution.

2. See results below:

Beetle mass /g	Tally	Total
2.1	I	1
2.2	II	2
2.4	II	2
2.5	IIII	4
2.6	III	3
2.7	I	1
2.8	II	2

Median = 8th value when in rank order = 2.5

Mode = 2.5

Mean = 2.49 ~ 2.5

Evaluating Your Results (page 33)

1. $H_2O_2 \rightarrow H_2 + O_2$

2. (a)-(c), completed table for mean, standard deviation, and rate below.

Stage	Mean	Std Dev	Mean rate / $cm^3\ s^{-1}\ g^{-1}$
0.5	10.1	0.5	0.03
2	34.9	3.8	0.12
4	65.5	5.0	0.22
6	36.7	4.0	0.12
10	22.5	2.7	0.08

3. (a) The values obtained for the 0.5 days and 10 days of germination are not in accordance with those obtained by the other groups (trials). The other values are of a similar magnitude.
   (b) If the new data are used, the mean should exclude those two values and be calculated using only 5 (rather than 6) trials for those germination stages.
   (c) These data values are clearly well adrift from the other values obtained for those stages from other groups (trial); if plotted as a scatter plot, they are distinct outliers on the plot. This suggests that something was wrong with either the measurement or the execution of the trial. It is reasonable therefore to exclude them from the analysis.

4. See below.

Catalase activity in relation to stage of germination in mung bean seedlings

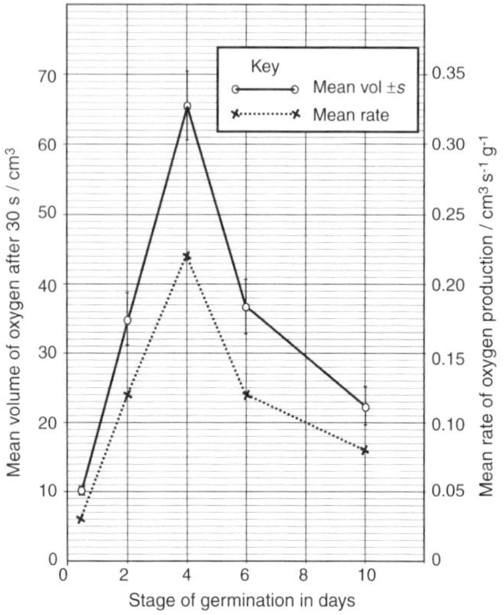

5. (a) The volume and rate of oxygen production increases rapidly to a peak at 4 days and declines, almost as sharply between 4 and 10 days.
   (b) Catalase activity in the sprouting seeds increases rapidly in the first 4 days of germination linked to the increase in cell activity and high respiration rates in early growth. It then falls off as the seedlings become established and metabolism slows.

6. Errors include: The equipment could potentially leak around the bung or the tubing. There could be a delay in delivering all the H_2O_2 so a slight delay in correctly timing the start of the reaction. The seeds might not be completely crushed, or crushed to different degrees so that not all the catalase is released.

7. Validity of data could be affected by (two of): insufficient usable data, variable data (overlapping data between times), old or poorly stored beans, old or poorly stored H_2O_2, precise and reliable data which was inaccurate because of gas losses through the equipment.

8. Improvements could include any one of: Using a mechanical grinder for a set period of time to ensure complete release of catalase. Using a petroleum sealant to prevent air leaks. Making sure the same person takes the measurement in each case, making sure all the trials are carried out with the same equipment by the same team.

KEY TERMS: Mix and Match (page 36)

Accuracy (Z), Bibliography (Y), Biological drawing (C), Citation (A), Control (G), Controlled variable (K), Data (D), Dependent variable (I), Graph (R), Histogram (L), Hypothesis (M), Independent variable (B), Mean (H), Measurement (P), Median (N), Mode (E), Observation (S), Parameter (BB), Precision (O), Qualitative data (U), Quantitative data (J), Raw data (Q), Reliability (X), Sample (V), Scientific method (T), Statistic (W), Trend (of data) (F), Variable (AA).

Cell Sizes (page 39)

1.

(a) *Amoeba*:	300 µm	0.3 mm
(b) Foraminiferan:	400 µm	0.4 mm
(c) *Leptospira*:	7-8 µm	0.007-0.008 mm
(d) Epidermis:	120 µm	0.12 mm
(e) *Daphnia*:	2500 µm	2.5 mm
(f) *Papillomavirus*:	0.13 µm	0.00013 mm

2. *Papillomavirus*; *Leptospira*; Epidermis (but not an organism); *Amoeba*; Foraminiferan; *Daphnia*

3. Onion epidermis (possibly); *Amoeba*; foraminiferan; *Daphnia*

4. (a) 0.00025 mm (b)0.45 mm (c) 0.0002 mm

Calculating Linear Magnification (page 40)

1. Actual size = image size ÷ magnification
   = 52 000 µm ÷ 140 = **400 µm (0.4 mm)**

2. (a) Actual length of scale line = 10 mm
   Stated length of scale line = 0.5 mm
   10 ÷ 0.5 = 20 X magnification
   (b) Measured length = 42 mm. Magnification = 20 X
   Actual length = 42 ÷ 20 = **2.1 mm**

3. 43 mm = 43 000 µm
   Magnification = size of the image ÷ actual size of object
   = 43 000 µm ÷ 2 µm = **21 500 X**

Optical Microscopes (page 41)

1. (a) Eyepiece lens
   (b) Arm
   (c) Coarse focus knob
   (d) Fine focus knob
   (e) Objective lens
   (f) Mechanical stage
   (g) Condenser
   (h) In-built light source
   (i) Eyepiece lens
   (j) Eyepiece focus
   (k) Focus knob
   (l) Objective lens
   (m) Stage

2. Phase contrast is used for transparent specimens (to increase contrast between transparent structures).

3. (a) Plant cell, any two of: Cell wall, nucleus (may see chromatin if stained appropriately), vacuole, cell membrane (high magnification), Golgi apparatus, mitochondria (high magnification), chloroplast, cytoplasm (if stained), nuclear envelope (maybe).
   (b) Animal cell, any two of: Nucleus (may see chromatin if stained appropriately), centriole, cell membrane (high magnification), Golgi apparatus, mitochondria (high magnification), cytoplasm (if stained).

4. Any of: Ribosomes, microtubules, endoplasmic reticulum, Golgi vesicles (free), nuclear envelope as two layers, lysosomes (animal cells). Also detail of organelles such as mitochondria and chloroplasts.

5. (a) Leishman's stain
   (b) Schultz's solution/iodine solution
   (c) Schultz's solution
   (d) Aniline sulfate/ Schultz's solution
   (e) Methylene blue
   (f) Schultz's solution

6. (a) 600X magnification (b) 600X magnification

7. Bright field, compound light microscopes produce a flat (2-dimensional) image from a thin, transparent sample. Dissecting microscopes produce a 3-dimensional image, revealing the surface details of the specimen.

8. Magnification is the number of times larger an image is than the specimen. Resolution is the degree of achievable detail. The limit of resolution is the minimum distance by which two points in a specimen can be separated and still be distinguished as separate.

Electron Microscopes (page 43)

1. The limit of resolution (see #8 above) is related to wavelength (about 0.45X the wavelength). The shortest visible light has a wavelength of about 450 nm giving a resolution of 0.45 x 450 nm; close to 200 nm. Points less than 200 nm apart will be perceived as one point or a blur. Electron beams have a shorter wavelength than light so the resolution is much greater (points 0.5 nm apart can be distinguished as separate points; a resolving power that is 400X that of a light microscope).

2. (a) **TEM**: Used to (any of): show cell ultrastructure i.e. organelles; to investigate changes in the number, size, shape, or condition of cells and organelles i.e. demonstrate cellular processes or activities; to detect the presence of viruses in cells.
   (b) **SEM**: Used to (any of): show the surface features of cells, e.g. guard cell surrounding a stoma; to show the surface features of organisms for identification (often used for invertebrates and viruses); for general identification by surface feature, e.g. for pollen used in palaeoclimate or forensic research.
   (c) **Bright field**: Used for (any of): examining prepared sections of tissue for cellular detail; for examining living tissue for large scale movements, e.g. blood flow in capillaries or cytoplasmic streaming.
   (d) **Dissecting**: Used for (any of): examining living specimens for surface detail and structures; sorting material from samples (e.g. leaf litter or stream invertebrates; dissecting a small organism where greater resolution than the naked eye is required.

3. A TEM
   B Bright field LM
   C TEM
   D Bright field LM
   E SEM
   F Bright field LM
   G Dissecting LM
   H SEM

Prokaryotic Cells (page 45)

1. (a) The nuclear material (DNA) is not contained within a clearly defined nucleus with a nuclear membrane.
   (b) Membrane-bound cellular organelles (e.g. mitochondria, endoplasmic reticulum) are missing.
   (c) Single, circular chromosome sometimes with accessory chromosomes called plasmids.

2. (a) Locomotion: Flagella enable bacterial movement out of unsuitable conditions to preferred conditions.
   (b) Fimbriae are shorter, straighter, and thinner than flagella. Used for attachment rather than locomotion.

3. (a) Bacterial cell wall lies outside the plasma (cell surface) membrane. It is a semi-rigid structure composed of a macromolecule called peptidoglycan, and contains varying amounts of lipopolysacchardies and lipoproteins.
   (b) The glycocalyx is a viscous, gelatinous layer lying outside the cell wall. It comprises polysaccharide and/or polypeptide, but not peptidoglycan, and may be firmly or loosely attached to the wall.

4. (a) Bacteria usually reproduce by binary fission, where the DNA replicates and the cell then splits into two.
   (b) Conjugation differs from binary fission in that DNA is exchanged between one bacterial cell (the donor) and another (the recipient). The recipient cell gains DNA from the donor.

5. Plasmids are used extensively in recombinant DNA technology. Being accessory to the main chromosome, the plasmid DNA can be manipulated easily. Using restriction enzymes, foreign genes (e.g. gene for producing insulin) can be spliced into a plasmid, which then carries out the instructions of the foreign gene.

Plant Cells (page 47)

1. A: Nucleus
   B: Cell wall
   C: Nucleus
   D: Chloroplasts

2. (a) The rapid movement of cytoplasm within eukaryotic cells, seen most clearly in plant and algal cells.
   (b)

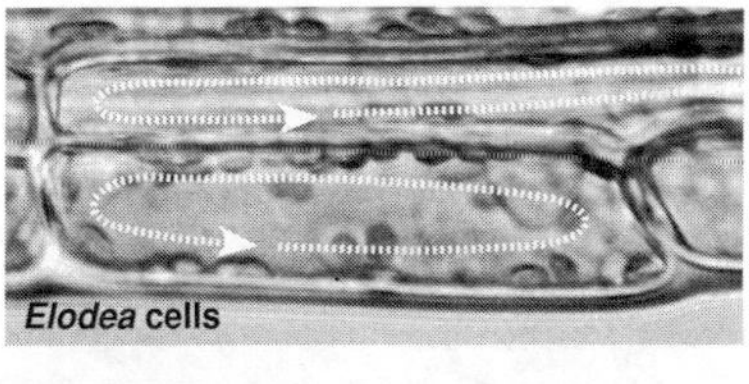

3. Any three of:
   - Starch (branched carbohydrate) granules stored in amyloplasts (energy store).
   - Chloroplasts, discrete plastids containing the pigment chlorophyll, involved in photosynthesis.
   - Large vacuole, often central (vacuoles are present in animal cells, but are only small).
   - Cell wall of cellulose forming the rigid, supporting structure outside the plasma membrane.
   - Plasmodesmata.

Animal Cells (page 48)

1. A: Nucleus B: Plasma membrane C: Nucleus
2. (a)

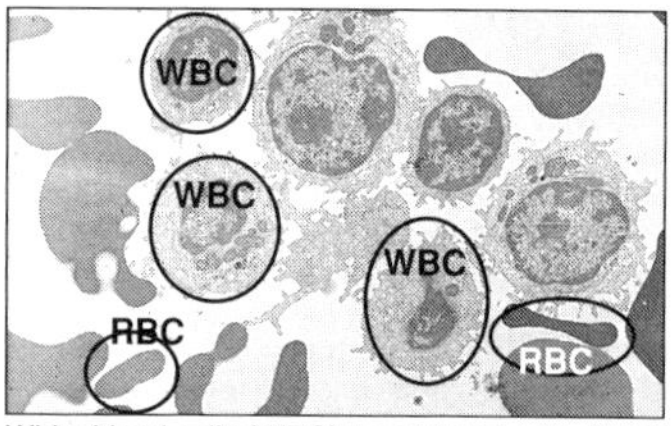

White blood cells (WBC) & red blood cells (RBC)

(b) Any of the following: RBCs have no nucleus and they are smaller than the white blood cells. White blood cells have extensions of the plasma membrane (associated with being phagocytic and mobile), are larger than RBCs, and have a nucleus.

3. Any one of:
   - Centrioles (although these are present in lower plants, they are absent from higher plants). They are microtubular structures responsible for forming the poles and the spindles during cell division.
   - Desmosomes. These are points of contact between the plasma membranes of neighbouring cells, which allow cells to combine together to form tissues.

The Cell's Cytoskeleton (page 49)

1. All components of the cytoskeleton are made up of protein subunits.
2. The dynamic nature is important because it enables movement of the cell and of materials within the cell, while resisting tension and providing structural support.
3. Cytoskeletal elements (microtubules and microfilaments) act as railroad tracks along which vesicles and organelles can move to specific places. This is an active process and carried out by motor proteins in the cell, which attach to the cytoskeletal elements and 'walk' materials along them.

Cell Structures and Organelles (page 50)

(b) **Name**: Ribosome
Location: Free in cytoplasm or bound to rough ER
Function: Synthesise polypeptides (=proteins)
Present in plant cells: Yes
Present in animal cells: Yes
Visible under LM: No

(c) **Name**: Mitochondrion
Location: In cytoplasm as discrete organelles
Function: Site of cellular respiration (ATP formation)
Present in plant cells: Yes
Present in animal cells: Yes
Visible under LM: Not with most standard school LM, but can be seen using high quality, high power LM.

(d) **Name**: Golgi apparatus
Location: In cytoplasm associated with the smooth endoplasmic reticulum, often close to the nucleus.
Function: Final modification of proteins and lipids. Sorting and storage for use in the cell or packaging molecules for export.
Present in plant cells: Yes
Present in animal cells: Yes
Visible under LM: Not with most standard school LM, but may be visible using high quality, high power LM.

(e) **Name**: Endoplasmic reticulum (in this case, rough ER)
Location: Penetrates the whole cytoplasm
Function: Involved in the transport of materials (e.g. proteins) within the cell and between the cell and its surroundings.
Present in plant cells: Yes
Present in animal cells: Yes
Visible under LM: No

(f) **Name**: Chloroplast
Location: Within the cytoplasm
Function: The site of photosynthesis
Present in plant cells: Yes
Present in animal cells: No
Visible under LM: Yes

(g) **Name**: Lysosome and food vacuole (given)
Lysosome
Location: Free in cytoplasm.
Function: Ingests and destroys foreign material. Able to digest the cell itself under some circumstances.
Present in plant cells: Yes but variably (vacuoles may have a lysosomal function in some plant cells).
Present in animal cells: Yes
Visible under LM: No

Vacuole (a food vacuole in an animal cell is shown, so students may answer with respect to this).
Location: In cytoplasm.
Function: In plant cells, the vacuole (often only one) is a large fluid filled structure involved in storage and support (turgor). In animal cells, vacuoles are smaller and more numerous, and are involved in storage (of water, wastes, and soluble pigments).
Present in plant cells: Yes, as (a) large structure(s).
Present in animal cells: Yes, smaller, more numerous
Visible under LM: Yes in plant cells, no in animal cells.

(h) **Name**: Nucleus
Location: Discrete organelle, position is variable.
Function: The control center of the cell; the site of the nuclear material (DNA).
Present in plant cells: Yes
Present in animal cells: Yes
Visible under LM: Yes.

(i) **Name**: Centrioles
Location: In cytoplasm, usually next to the nucleus.
Function: Involved in cell division (probably in the organisation of the spindle fibers).
Present in plant cells: Variably (absent in higher plants)
Present in animal cells: Yes
Visible under LM: No.

(j) **Name**: Cilia and flagella (given)
Location: Anchored in the cell membrane and extending outside the cell.

Function: Motility.
Present in plant cells: No
Present in animal cells: Yes
Visible under LM: Variably (depends on magnification and preparation/fixation of material).

(k) **Name**: Cytoskeleton
Location: Throughout cytoplasm
Function: Provides structure and shape to a cell, responsible for cell movement (e.g. during muscle contraction), and provides intracellular transport of organelles and other structures.
Present in plant cells: Yes
Present in animal cells: Yes
Visible under LM: No

(l) **Name**: Cellulose cell wall
Location: Surrounds the cell and lies outside the plasma membrane.
Function: Provides rigidity and strength, and supports the cell against changes in turgor.
Present in plant cells: Yes
Present in animal cells: No
Visible under LM: Yes

(m) **Name**: Cell junctions (an animal example is given)
Location: At cell membrane surface, connecting adjacent cells.
Function: Depends on junction type. Desmosomes fasten cells together, gap junctions act as communication channels between cells, and tight junctions prevent leakage of extracellular fluid from layers of epithelial cells.
Present in plant cells: Yes, as plasmodesmata
Present in animal cells: Yes
Visible under LM: No

Packaging Proteins (page 53)

1. Large organic polymers made up of many repeating units of smaller molecules. They have a high molecular weight. Examples include proteins and nucleic acids.
2. Polypeptides are synthesised by membrane bound ribosomes so that they can be easily threaded through the ER membrane into the cisternal space of the ER. Here they are in place for subsequent modification, packaging and export.
3. The carbohydrates attached to glycoproteins aid in the recognition or function of the protein so that it is transported to the correct destination and performs its appropriate functional role.
4. (a) Rough ER: Ribosomes on the rough ER assemble the proteins destined for secretion.
(b) Smooth ER: Synthesis of lipids, e.g. steroid hormones and phospholipids, and packages them into transport vesicles.
(c) Golgi apparatus: Receives transport vesicles. Modifies, stores, and transports molecules for export around or from the cell.
(d) Transport vesicles: These bud off the ER and move substances to the Golgi apparatus.

Interpreting Electron Micrographs (page 54)

1. (a) Lysosome
(b) Animal cells (the equivalent functions in plant cells and yeast is performed by lytic vacuoles).
(c) Contains hydrolytic enzymes to digest excess or worn-out organelles, food particles, and engulfed viruses or bacteria.
2. (a) Golgi apparatus
(b) Plant and animal cells
(c) Function: Packages substances to be secreted by the cell. Forms a membrane vesicle containing the chemicals for export from the cell (e.g. nerve cells export neurotransmitters; endocrine glands export hormones; digestive gland cells export enzymes).
3. (a) Mitochondrion
(b) Plant and animal cells (most common in cells that have high energy demands, such as muscle).
(c) Function: Site of most of the process of cellular respiration, which releases energy from food (glucose) to fuel metabolism.
(d)

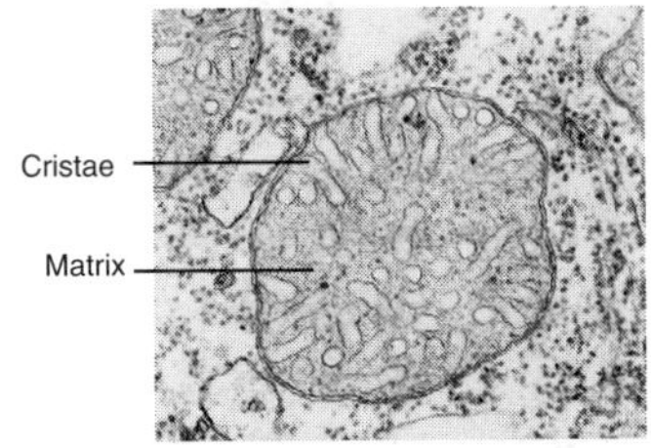

4. (a) Endoplasmic reticulum
(b) Plant and animal cells (eukaryotes)
(c) Function: Site of protein synthesis (translation stage). Transport network that moves substances through its system of tubes. Many complex reactions need to take place on the surface of the membranes.
(d) Ribosomes.
5. (a) Nucleus
(b) Plant and animal cells (eukaryotes)
(c) Function: Controls cell metabolism and functioning of the whole organism. These instructions are inherited from one generation to the next.
(d)

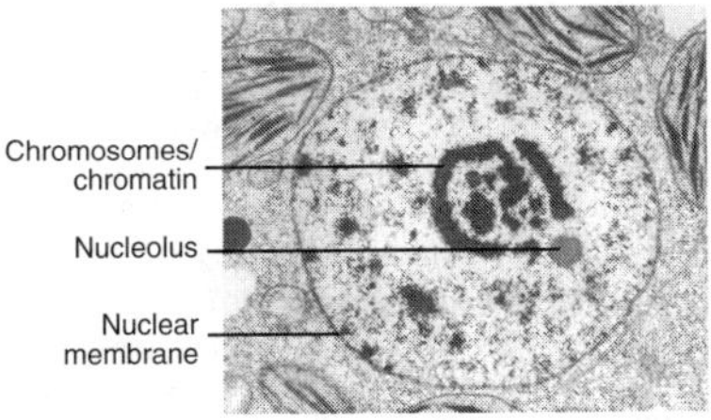

Identifying Structures in an Animal Cell (page 55)

1. (a) Plasma membrane
(b) Rough ER
(c) Centriole (TS)
(d) Mitochondrion
(e) Lysosome
(f) Nucleus
(g) Golgi aparatus
(h) Cytoplasm
2. Centrioles
3. Plant cells are enclosed by a rigid cellulose cell

wall and do not have the capacity for motility or phagocytosis in the way that animal cells do.

4. (a) Protein production and secretion indicated by a large amount of ER and an extensive Golgi.
   (b) Large number of mitochondria indicate that it is metabolically very active (high respiration rate).

5. It has a membrane-bound nucleus and membrane-bound organelles.

Identifying Plant Cell Structures (page 56)

1. (a) Cytoplasm
   (b) Vacuole
   (c) Starch granule
   (d) Chloroplast
   (e) Mitochondria
   (f) Cell wall
   (g) Chromosome
   (h) Nuclear membrane
   (i) Endoplasmic reticulum
   (j) Plasma membrane

2. 9 cells (1 complete cell, plus the edges of 8 others)

3. Chloroplasts, cell wall, highly geometric cell shape.

4. (a) Cytoplasm located between the plasma membrane and nuclear membrane (extranuclear).
   (b) Composition of cytoplasm: A watery soup of dissolved substances. In eukaryotic cells, organelles are found in the cytoplasm. Cytoplasm = cytosol (including cytoskeleton) + organelles.
   (c) Prokaryotic cells do not have a defined nucleus.

5. (a) Starch granules, which occur in specialised plastids called leucoplasts. Starch granules are non-living inclusions, deposited as a reserve energy store.
   (b) Vacuoles, which are fluid filled cavities bounded by a single membrane. Plant vacuoles contain cell sap; an aqueous solution of dissolved food material, ions, waste products, and pigments. **Note**: Young plant cells (such as the one pictured) usually have several small vacuoles, which unite in a mature cell to form a large, permanent central vacuole.

How Do We Know? Membrane Structure (page 57)

1. Fixing a sample and then freezing it preserves its structure and allows it to be cleaved. The cleavage (splitting) process reveals internal structure. The techniques used in freeze fracture (splitting a lipid bilayer) and electron microscopy (coating in metals) reveal how proteins are organised in the membrane.

2. The impressions left in one side of the membrane after freeze fracture give evidence of proteins located within the membrane. Fracturing the membrane allowed scientists to observe the presence of integral membrane proteins which span the membrane lipid bilayer. This supported the fluid mosaic model, in which membrane bound proteins are able to move relatively freely within the membrane.

3. If the bilayer had a continuous protein coat, the freeze fracture specimen would look flat and uniform when viewed under the electron microscope.
   The proteins are discrete complexes randomly spaced throughout the lipid bilayer. The bumps observed are where the proteins were located.

The Structure of Membranes (page 59)

1. (a) Channel proteins and some carrier proteins.
   (b) Carrier proteins (ion pumps)
   (c) Glycoproteins and glycolipids
   (d) Cholesterol

2. (a) Membranes are composed of a phospholipid bilayer in which are embedded proteins, glycoproteins, and glycolipids. The structure is relatively fluid and the proteins are able to move within this fluid matrix.
   (b) This model accounts for the properties we observe in cellular membranes: its **fluidity** (how its shape is not static and how its components move within the membrane, relative to one-another) and its **mosaic nature** (the way in which the relative proportions of the membrane components, i.e. proteins, glycoproteins, glycolipids etc, can vary from membrane to membrane). The fluid mosaic model also accounts for how membranes can allow for the selective passage of materials (through protein channels for example) and how they enable cell-cell recognition (again, as a result of membrane components such as glycoproteins).

3. Membranes perform many diverse roles. The plasma membrane forms the outer limit of the cell and contains the proteins that confer cellular recognition. It also controls the entry and exit of materials into and out of the cell. Intracellular membranes keep the cytoplasm separate from the extracellular spaces and provide compartments within cells for localisation of metabolic (enzymatic) reactions. They also provide a surface for the attachment of the enzymes involved in metabolism.

4. (a) Any of: Golgi, mitochondria, chloroplasts, nucleus, endoplasmic reticulum, vacuoles, lysosomes.
   (b) Depends on choice: Generally the membrane's purpose is to compartmentalise the location of enzymatic reactions, to control the entry and exit of substances that the organelle operates on, and/or to provide a surface for enzyme attachment.

5. (a) Cholesterol lies between the phospholipids and prevents close packing. It thus functions to keep membranes more fluid. The greater the amount of cholesterol in the membrane the greater its fluidity.
   (b) At temperatures close to freezing, high proportions of membrane cholesterol is important in keeping membranes fluid and functioning.

6. (a)-(c) in any order: Oxygen, food (glucose), minerals and trace elements, water.

7. (a) Carbon dioxide (b) Nitrogenous wastes

8.

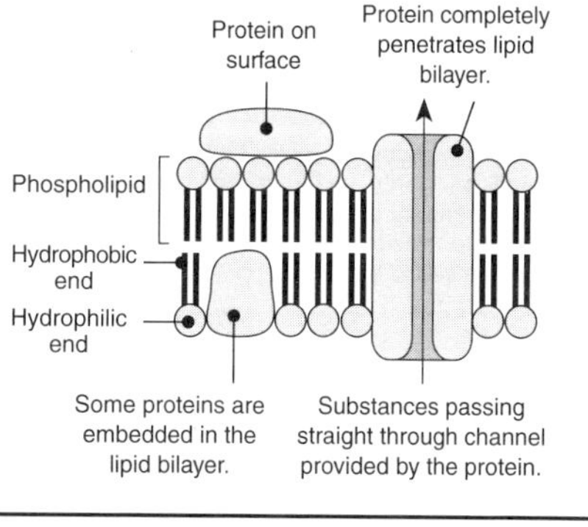

The Role of Membranes in Cells (page 61)

1. (a) Compartments within cells allow specific metabolic pathways in the cell to be localised. This achieves greater efficiency of cell function and restricts potentially harmful reactions and substances (e.g. hydrogen peroxide) to specific areas.
   (b) Greater membrane surface area provides a greater area over which membrane-bound reactions can occur. This increases the speed and efficiency with which metabolic reactions can take place.

2. (a) Golgi apparatus
   (b) lysosome
   (c) mitochondrion
   (d) rough endoplasmic reticulum
   (e) smooth endoplasmic reticulum
   (f) chloroplast

3. Membrane surface area is increased within cells and organelles by invaginations or by a long flattened shape which increases the surface area to volume ratio.

4. (a) High membrane surface area provides a greater area over which membrane-bound reactions can occur. This increases the speed and efficiency with which metabolic reactions can take place.
   (b) Channel and carrier proteins facilitate selective transport of substances through membranes. They can help to speed up the transport of substances into and out of the cell, especially for enzymatic reactions requiring a steady supply of substrate and constant removal of end-product, e.g. ADP supply to the mitochondrion during cellular respiration.

5. (a) Non-polar (lipid-soluble) molecules are able to dissolve in the lipid bilayer structure of the membrane and diffuse easily into the cell whereas the polar (lipid-insoluble) molecules have to be actively transported through the membrane.
   (b) Transport of lipid-soluble molecules into cells by diffusion is relatively quick compared to transport of lipid-insoluble molecules, which that have to be actively transported across the plasma membrane.

Cell Signalling and Receptors (page 63)

1. Cell signalling is a complex communication system by which cells gather information (chemical signals) about their environment, and change their cellular activity accordingly to respond to it. Cell signalling is also enables communication between cells.

2. (a) Endocrine signalling (b) Paracrine signalling

3. All cell signalling mechanisms have in common some kind of chemical messenger or signal molecule (ligand) and a receptor molecule (on the target cells, which may or may not be on the cell producing the signal).

4. (a) Hormone binding receptors initiate a series of reactions within the cell that result in a physiological change, often to maintain homeostasis. In many cases hormones exert their effects by influencing genes directly or the enzymes associated with membranes. For example, when the hormone insulin binds to a membrane receptor, the cell's glucose transporters open and glucose is taken up from the blood and used for metabolism or storage.
   (b) The binding of a drug to a membrane receptor initiates a physiological response. Two responses by the cell are common. Agonistic drugs cause a stimulatory effect on the cell, while antagonistic drugs block or depress aspects of the cell's activity.

Passive Transport Processes (page 64)

1. (a) Large surface area (b) Thin membrane

2. (a) and (b) any of:
   - Molecules always move down a concentration gradient (from high to low concentration).
   - Molecules diffuse along their own concentration gradient, independent of other molecules (so two way diffusion is common in biological systems).
   - Diffusion rates are higher at higher temperatures.
   - Diffusion rates are faster when the concentration gradient is greater.
   - Thicker barriers slow diffusion.

3. (a) Channel-mediated facilitated diffusion, i.e through a protein channel in the membrane that creates a hydrophilic pore.
   (b) Carrier mediated facilitated diffusion, i.e. the molecule is aided across the membrane by a carrier protein specific to the molecule being transported.

4. Concentration gradients are maintained by (any one of): Constant use or transport away of a substance on one side of a membrane (e.g. use of ADP in mitochondria). Production of a substance on one side of a membrane (e.g. production of CO_2 by respiring cells).

5. Aquaporins are protein channels in the membrane specific to water molecules. This is faster (less resistance) than diffusion through the membrane.

6. (a) Zero
   (b) It water potential becomes more negative (lower)
   (c) Uptake of sucrose into the phloem (water follows passively by osmosis).

7. (a) -100 → -200 water moves to cell on the right
   (b) -400 ↔ -400 no net movement
   (a) -400 ← -200 water moves to the cell on the left

8. The fluid replacement should have a less negative water potential than the body fluids. Fluid replacements must induce the movement of water into the cells and tissues (which are dehydrated and therefore have a more negative water potential than the drink).

9. (a) Pressure potential generated within plant cells provides the turgor necessary for keeping unlignified plant tissues supported.
   (b) Without cell turgor, soft plant tissues (soft stems and flower parts for example) would lose support and wilt. Note that some tissues are supported by structural components such as lignin.

10. Animal cells are less robust than plant cells against changes in net water content: Excess influx will cause bursting and excess loss causes crenulation.

11. (a) Water will move into the cell and it will burst (lyse).
    (b) The cell would lose water and the plasma membrane would crinkle up (crenulate).
    (c) Water will move into the cell and it will burst (lyse).

Ion Pumps (page 67)

1. ATP (directly or indirectly) supplies the energy to move substances against their concentration gradient.

2. (a) Cotransport describes coupling the movement of a molecule (such as sucrose or glucose) against its concentration gradient to the diffusion of an ion (e.g. H^+ or Na^+) down its concentration gradient. Note: An energy requiring ion exchange pump is used to establish this concentration gradient.
   (b) In the gut, a gradient in sodium ions is used to drive the transport of glucose across the epithelium. A Na^+/K^+ pump (requiring ATP) establishes an unequal concentration of Na^+ across the membrane. A specific membrane protein then couples the return of Na^+ down its concentration gradient to the transport of glucose (at a rate that is higher than could occur by diffusion alone).
   (c) The glucose diffuses from the epithelial cells of the gut into the blood, where it is transported away. This maintains a low level in the intestinal epithelial cells.

3. Extracellular accumulation of Na^+ (any two of):
   - maintains the gradient that is used to cotransport useful molecules, such as glucose, into cells.
   - maintains cell volume by creating an osmotic gradient that drives the absorption of water.
   - establishes and maintains resting potential in nerve and muscle cells.
   - provides the driving force for several facilitated membrane transport proteins.

Exocytosis and Endocytosis (page 68)

1. **Phagocytosis** is the engulfment of solid material by endocytosis whereas **pinocytosis** is the uptake of liquids or fine suspensions by endocytosis.

2. Phagocytosis examples (any of):
   • Feeding in *Amoeba* by engulfment of material using cytoplasmic extensions called pseudopodia. • Ingestion of old red blood cells by Kupffer cells in the liver. • Ingestion of bacteria and cell debris by neutrophils and macrophages (phagocytic white blood cells).

3. Exocytosis examples (any of):
   • Secretion of substances from specialised secretory cells in multicellular organisms, e.g. hormones from endocrine cells, digestive secretions from exocrine cells. • Expulsion of wastes from unicellular organisms, e.g. *Paramecium* and *Amoeba* expelling residues from food vacuoles.

4. Any type of cytosis (unlike diffusion) is an active process involving the use of ATP. Low oxygen inhibits oxidative metabolism and lowers the energy yield from the respiration of substrates (ATP availability drops).

5. (a) **Oxygen**: Diffusion.
   (b) **Cellular debris**: Phagocytosis.
   (c) **Water**: Osmosis.
   (d) **Glucose**: Facilitated diffusion.

Active and Passive Transport Summary (page 69)

1. A. Diffusion
   B. Osmosis
   C. Facilitated diffusion
   D. Ion pump (or sodium-potassium pump)
   E. Pinocytosis
   F. Exocytosis
   G. Phagocytosis

2. **Passive transport** requires no energy input from the cell; materials follow a concentration gradient.
   Active transport requires considerable amounts of energy (ATP) to make materials go in a direction they would not normally go (at least at the rate required).

3. Gases moving by **diffusion**: Oxygen, carbon dioxide.

4. (a) Pinocytosis
   (b) Phagocytosis.
   (c) Osmosis
   (d) Exocytosis
   (e) Receptor-mediated endocytosis (see page 68)
   (f) Phagocytosis
   (g) Facilitated diffusion
   (h) Carrier-mediated facilitated diffusion (see page 64)
   (i) Sodium-potassium pump

KEY TERMS: Mix and Match (page 70)

Active transport (F), Amphipathic (O), Aquaporin (Y), Cell signalling (AA), Channel proteins (T), Cncentration gradient (S), Diffusion (M), Endocytosis (R), Exocytosis (V), Facilitated diffusion (C), Fluid mosaic model (B), Glycolipids (J), Glycoproteins (U), Ionophore (Z), Ion pump (Q), Osmosis (A), Paracrine (L), Partially permeable membrane (W), Passive transport (N), Phagocytosis (G), Plasma membrane (P), Plasmolysis (E), Pressure potential (H), Solute potential (X), Surface area: volume ratio (K), Turgor (I), Water potential (D).

Cell Division (page 72)

1. (a) Mitosis: Cell division for growth and repair produces cells with 2N chromosome number.
   (b) Meiosis: Cell division for producing gametes (sperm, eggs) and spores with 1N chromosome number.

2. In **spermatogenesis**, the nucleus of the germ cell divides twice to produce four similar sized gametes (sperm cells). In **oogenesis**, the two divisions are not equal and only one of the four nuclei (and most of the cytoplasm) produce the egg cell.

3. In humans, gametes are produced by meiotic division from diploid cells. In plants, gametes are produced by mitosis from haploid gametophytes.

Mitosis and the Cell Cycle (page 73)

1. A. Anaphase
   B. Prophase
   C. Late metaphase (early anaphase also acceptable).
   D. Late anaphase
   E. Cytokinesis (late telophase is also acceptable).

2. Replicate the DNA to form a second chromatid.
   Coil up into visible chromosomes to avoid tangling.

3. A. Interphase: The stage between cell divisions (mitoses). Just before mitosis, the DNA is replicated to form an extra copy of each chromosome (still part of the same chromosome as an extra chromatid).
   B. Late prophase: Chromosomes condense (coil and fold up) into visible form. Centrioles move to

opposite ends of the cell.
C. Metaphase: Spindle fibers form between the centrioles. Chromosomes attach to the spindle fibers at the cell 'equator'.
D. Late anaphase: Chromatids from each chromosome are pulled apart and move in opposite directions, towards the centrioles.
E. Telophase: Chromosomes begin to unwind again. Two new nuclei form. The cell plate forms across the midline where the new cell wall will form.
F. Cytokinesis: Cell cytoplasm divides to create two distinct 'daughter cells' from the original cell. It is in this form for most of its existence, and carries out its designated role (normal function).

Differentiation of Human Cells (page 75)

1. (a) Self renewal while remaining unspecialised.
   (b) Potency, the ability to differentiate into any number of specialised cells

2. Embryonic stem cells are pluripotent and can form any cells derived from the three germ layers. Adult stem cells are multipotent; they are more limited in the numbers of cells that they can form, and generally form the cells of the blood, heart, muscle, and nerves. Embryonic stem cells have far greater medical potential because of their ability to form all cell types. They potentially could be used for regenerative medicine and tissue replacement.

3. Adult stem cells are often involved in replacement of dying cells and the repair of damaged tissue. Students may provide any one of the following examples to illustrate the role of adult stem cells:

- Hematopoietic stem cells,from bone marrow, regenerate all blood cell types to replace old or damaged cells.
- Bone marrow stromal cells (mesenchymal stem cells) give rise to a variety of cell types: bone cells (osteocytes), cartilage cells (chondrocytes), fat cells (adipocytes), and other kinds of connective tissue cells such as those in tendons.
- Neural stem cells in the brain give rise to three major cell types: neurones, astrocytes, and oligodendrocytes.
- Epithelial stem cells in the lining of the digestive tract are continually producing cells to replace those damaged during the digestive process. Cell types include absorptive cells, goblet cells, Paneth cells, and enteroendocrine cells.
- Skin stem cells give rise to keratinocytes, which migrate to the skin surface and are regenerated frequently to replace old or damaged cells and maintain a protective layer. Follicular stem cells at the base of hair follicles give rise to the hair follicle and epidermal cells.

4. Advantages of using embryonic stem cell cloning in tissue engineering (any one for achieved):

- This technology will provide a disease-free and plentiful supply of (tissue-typed, compatible) cells.
- Embryonic stem cells have the ability to develop and form all the tissues of the body. Theoretically, there should be no shortage of specific cell types.
- It will improve the possibility of creating semi-synthetic living organs for use as replacement parts.

Human Cell Specialisation (page 76)

1. (b) **Erythrocyte**:
   Features: Biconcave cell, lacking mitochondria, nucleus, and most internal membranes. Contains the oxygen-transporting pigment, haemoglobin.
   Role: Uptake, transport, and release of oxygen to the tissues. Some transport of CO_2. Lack of organelles creates more space for oxygen transport. Lack of mitochondria prevents oxygen use.
   (c) **Retinal rod (photoreceptor) cell**:
   Features: Long, narrow cell with light-sensitive pigment (rhodopsin) embedded in the membranes.
   Role: Detection of light: light causes a structural change in the membranes and leads to a nerve impulse (result is visual perception).
   (d) **Skeletal muscle cell**:
   Features: Cylindrical shape with banded myofibrils. Capable of contraction (shortening).
   Role: Move voluntary muscles acting on skeleton.
   (e) **Intestinal goblet cell (secretory cell)**:
   Features: Flask-shaped cell with basal nucleus and a cell interior filled with mucus globules.
   Role: Secrete mucus to protect the epithelium from abrasion and from the action of digestive enzymes.
   (f) **Motor neurone cell**:
   Features: Cell body with a long extension (the axon) ending in synaptic bodies. Axon is insulated with a sheath of fatty material (myelin).
   Role: Rapid conduction of motor nerve impulses from the spinal cord to effectors (e.g. muscle).
   (g) **Spermatocyte**:
   Features: Motile, flagellated cell with mitochondria. Nucleus forms a large proportion of the cell.
   Role: Male gamete for sexual reproduction. Mitochondria provide the energy for motility.
   (h) **Osteocyte**:
   Features: Cell with calcium matrix around it. Fingerlike extensions enable the cell to be supplied with nutrients and wastes to be removed.
   Role: In early stages, secretes the matrix that will be the structural component of bone. Provides strength.

Differentiation of Plant Cells (page 77)

1. The meristems in plants consist of undifferentiated cells and cell division in the meristems provide new cells for expansion and differentiation of tissues.

2. Primary meristems are located in apical regions, i.e. the growing tips of the shoots and roots. Primary meristems are responsible for an increase in length or height. Some plants also have secondary meristems (the vascular cambium) encircling the stem, which produces increase in plant girth (diameter).

3. Meristematic tissue comprises undifferentiated cells (it is equivalent to stem cells in animals).

4. Primary tissues are formed from the primary meristems. Three primary meristems are produced from the apical meristem. The protoderm forms the epidermis, the ground meristem forms pith, cortex, and mesophyll, while the procambium leads to the formation of primary phloem and xylem. These form vascular bundles.

Plant Cell Specialisation (page 78)

1. (b) **Pollen grain**:
   Features: Small, lightweight, often with spikes.
   Role: houses male gamete for sexual reproduction.
   (c) **Palisade parenchyma cell**:
   Features: Column-shaped cell with chloroplasts.
   Role: Primary photosynthetic cells of the leaf.
   (d) **Epidermal cell**:
   Features: Waxy surface on a flat-shaped cell.
   Role: Provides a barrier to water loss on leaf.
   (e) **Vessel element**:
   Features: Rigid remains of a dead cell. No cytoplasm. End walls perforated. Walls are strengthened with lignin fibres.
   Role: Rapid conduction of water through the stem. Provides support for stem/trunk.
   (f) **Stone cell**:
   Features: Very thick lignified cell wall inside the primary cell wall. The cytoplasm is restricted to a small central region of the cell.
   Role: Protection of the seed inside the fruit.
   (g) **Sieve tube member**:
   Features: Long, tube-shaped cell without a nucleus. Cytoplasm continuous with other sieve cells above and below it. Cytoplasmic streaming is evident.
   Role: Responsible for translocation of sugars etc.
   (h) **Root hair cell:**
   Features: Thin cuticle with no waxy layer. High surface area relative to volume.
   Role: Facilitates the uptake of water and ions.

Root Cell Development (page 79)

1. (a) Cells specialise to take on specific functions.
   (b) Cells are becoming longer and/or larger.
   (c) Cells are dividing by mitosis.

2. (a) Late anaphase; chromatids are being pulled apart and are at opposite poles.
   (b) Telophase; there are two new nuclei formed and the cell plate is visible.
   (c) 25 of 250 cells were in mitosis, therefore mitosis occupies 25/250 or one tenth of the cell cycle.

3. The **cambium layer** of cells (lying under the bark between the outer phloem layer of cells and the inner xylem layer of cells). **Note**: Cells dividing from each side of this layer specialise to form new phloem on the outside and new xylem on the inside.

Levels of Organisation (page 80)

1. **Animals**
   (a) **Molecular**: Adrenaline, collagen, DNA, phospholipid
   (b) **Organelles**: Lysosome, ribosomes
   (c) **Cells**: Leucocyte, mast cell, neurone, Schwann cell
   (d) **Tissues**: Blood, bone, cardiac muscle, cartilage, squamous epithelium
   (e) **Organs**: Brain, heart, spleen
   (f) **Organ system**: Nervous system, reproductive system

2. **Plants**
   (a) **Molecular**: Pectin, cellulose, DNA, phospholipid
   (b) **Organelles**: Chloroplasts, ribosomes
   (c) **Cells**: Companion cells, epidermal cell, fibres, tracheid
   (d) **Tissues**: Collenchyma*, mesophyll, parenchyma*, phloem, sclerenchyma
   (e) **Organs**: Flowers, leaf, roots

   * **Note**: Parenchyma and collenchyma are simple tissues comprising only one type of cell (parenchyma and collenchyma cells respectively). Simple plant tissues are usually identified by cell name alone.

Animal Tissues (page 81)

1. The organisation of cells into specialised tissues allows the tissues to perform particular functions. This improves efficiency of function because different tasks can be shared amongst specialised cells. Energy is saved in not maintaining non-essential organelles in cells that do not require them.

2. (a) **Stratified squamous epithelium**: Lines organs but more durable (being many layers) than simple epithelium, e.g. skin and vagina.
   (b) **Simple squamous epithleium**: Single layer lining surfaces across which rapid diffusion is needed, e.g. lining the glomerular capsule, and the endothelium of the alveoli and the capillaries.
   (c) **Ciliated epithelium**: Specialised to move material out of passages, e.g. lining the nasal passages and the bronchus.
   (d) **Glandular epithelium**: Specialised to produced secretions either to lubricate surfaces or export substances (such as digestive secretions). It forms the covering of all the major glands and is also present in the intestinal lining.

3. (a) Ciliated cells with hair-like outgrowths that beat rhythmically to move mucus along.
   (b) Very thin, squamous (flattened) cells, across which substances can diffuse rapidly.

Plant Tissues (page 82)

1. **Collenchyma**
   Cell type(s): collenchyma cells
   Role: provides flexible support.

   Sclerenchyma
   Cell type(s): sclerenchyma cells
   Role: provides rigid, hard support.

   Root Endodermis
   Cell type(s): endodermal cells
   Role: Provides selective barrier regulating the passage of substances from the soil to the vascular tissue.

   Pericycle
   Cell type(s): parenchyma cells
   Role: Production of branch roots, synthesis and transport of alkaloids.

   Leaf mesophyll
   Cell type(s): spongy mesophyll, palisade mesophyll
   Role: Main photosynthesis site in the plant.

   Xylem
   Cell type(s): tracheids, vessel members, fibers, paraenchyma cells
   Role: Conducts water and dissolved minerals in vascular plants.

   Phloem
   Cell type(s): sieve-tube members, companion cells, parenchyma, fibers, sclereids
   Role: transport of dissolved organic material (including sugars) within vascular plants.

Epidermis
Cell type(s): epidermal cells, guard cells, subsidiary cells, and epidermal hairs (trichomes).
Role: Protection against water loss, regulation of gas exchange, secretion, water and mineral absorption.

KEY TERMS: Word Find (page 83)

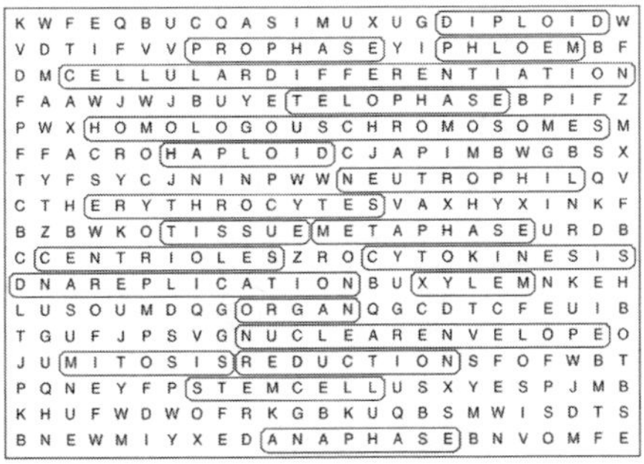

The Need for Gas Exchange (page 85)

1. **Cellular respiration** refers to the production of ATP through the oxidation of glucose. **Gas exchange** refers to the way in which respiratory gases (oxygen and carbon dioxide) are exchanged with the environment. Oxygen is required to drive the reactions of cellular respiration. Carbon dioxide is a waste product.

2. (a) Large surface area to provide for a large amount of gas exchange (to meet the organism's needs).
   (b) Thin membrane that does not present a large barrier to diffusion of gases.
   (c) Associated with mechanisms (e.g. blood flow) to maintain the concentration gradient.

3. The rate of diffusion across the gas exchange surface will be more rapid when membrane surface area or concentration difference across the membrane increases and/or membrane thickness decreases.

Why a Gas Exchange System? (page 86)

1. (a) Provides adequate supply and removal of respiratory gases necessary for an active (metabolically demanding) lifestyle.
   (b) Enables animals to attain a larger size (as they are freed from a dependence on direct diffusion of gases across thin body surfaces).

2. (a) Air breathers produce mucus that keeps the gas exchange surface moist.
   (b) Some water vapour is present in lungs as a result of metabolism.

3. (a) and (b) any two in any order:
   - In birds, air sacs function in ventilating the lungs (where gas exchange occurs). They facilitate one way (rather than to and fro) flow of air through the lung tissue.
   - Increased surface area provided through extensive branching of bronchioles and a large number of alveoli in mammals.
   - Active ventilation of the gas exchange surface (opercular movement in bony fish, constant swimming in sharks, breathing in birds, reptiles, amphibians, and mammals).
   - High oxygen extraction rates achieved through countercurrent exchange in fish gills.

Surface Area and Volume (page 87)

1.

Cube	Surface Area	Volume	Ratio
3 cm:	3 x 3 x 6 = 54	3 x 3 x 3 = 27	2.0 to 1
4 cm:	4 x 4 x 6 = 96	4 x 4 x 4 = 64	1.5 to 1
5 cm:	5 x 5 x 6 = 150	5 x 5 x 5 = 125	1.2 to 1

2. Surface area to volume graph: see the next column:

3. Volume

4. Increasing size leads to less surface area for a given volume. The surface area to volume ratio decreases.

5. Less surface area at the cell surface. This is the gas exchange surface, so large cells will have difficulty moving enough materials in and out of the cell to meet demands. This is what limits a cell's maximum size.
   Note: Eukaryote cells are typically about 0.01-0.1 mm in size, but some can be bigger than 1 mm. The largest cell is the female sex cell (ovum) of the ostrich, which averages 15-20 cm in length. Technically a single cell, it is atypical in size because almost the entire mass of the egg is food reserve in the form of yolk.

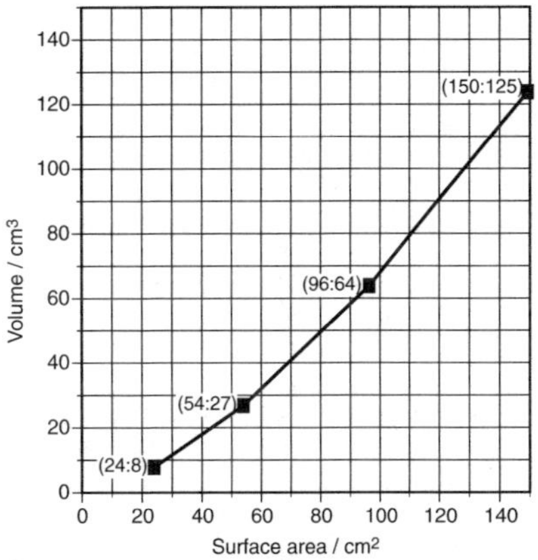

Breathing in Humans (page 89)

1. Breathing ventilates the lungs, renewing the supply of fresh (high oxygen) air while expelling high carbon dioxide air (CO_2 gained as a result of gas exchanges in the tissues).

2. (a) Quiet breathing: External intercostal muscles and diaphragm contract. Lung space increases and air flows into the lungs (inspiration). Inflation is detected and breath in ends. Expiration occurs through elastic recoil of the ribcage and lung tissue (air flows passively out to equalise with outside air pressure).
   (b) During forced or active breathing, muscular contraction is involved in both the inspiration and the expiration (expiration is not passive).

3. Water vapour
4. The elasticity of the lung tissue enables natural recoil of the lungs during quiet breathing so that expiration is a passive process not requiring energy.
5. Blood pH is a good indicator of high carbon dioxide levels, since increased CO_2 levels cause blood pH to fall. This indicates a need to increase respiratory rate to remove the CO_2 (and obtain more oxygen).

Responses to Exercise (page 90)

1. (a) Oxygen consumption increases twenty times or more. Most of this increase occurs in the muscle.
   (b) The gas exchange system responses by increasing the rate and depth of breathing (to deliver more oxygen and remove the carbon dioxide).
2. (a) Cardiac output increases more than five times.
   (b) As with the gas exchange system, the heart responds to the increased demand for oxygen by increasing its output to increase the rate at which exchanges can occur between the blood and working tissues (muscles).
3. (a) Training improves the efficiency of ventilation.
   (b) As a consequence of these adjustments, training improves the capacity for exercise. For any given exercise level, the ventilation response to exercise is reduced - exercise feels easier.

The Human Gas Exchange System (page 91)

1. (a) The structural arrangement (lobes, each with its own bronchus and dividing many times before terminating in numerous alveoli) provides an immense surface area for gas exchange.
   (b) Gas exchange takes place in the alveoli.
2. The alveolar-capillary membrane is the layered junction between the alveolar cells, the endothelial cells of the capillaries, and their associated basement membranes. It provides a surface across which gases can move freely by diffusion.
3. Surfactant reduces the surface tension of the lung tissue and counteracts the tendency of the alveoli to recoil inward and stick together after each expiration.
4. Completed table as below:

	Region	Cartilage	Ciliated epithelium	Goblet cells (mucus)	Smooth muscle	Connective tissue
1	Trachea	✓	✓	✓	✓	✓
2	Bronchus	✓	✓	✓	✓	✓
3	Bronchioles	gradually lost	✓	✓	✓	✓
4	Alveolar duct	✗	✗	✗	✓	✓
5	Alveoli	✗	✗	✗	very little	✓

5. Respiratory distress syndrome: The lack of surfactant and high surface tension in the alveoli result in the collapse of the lungs to an uninflated state after each breath. Breathing is difficult and laboured, oxygen delivery is inadequate and, if untreated, death usually follows in a few hours.

Measuring Lung Function (page 93)

1. (a) Taller people generally have larger lung volumes and capacities.
   (b) Males have larger lung volumes and capacities than females.
   (c) After adulthood, lung volume and capacity declines with age. Children have smaller lung volumes and lung capacities than adults.
2. (a) Forced volume is a more useful indicator of impairment of lung function than a tidal volume because people use only a small proportion of their lung volume in normal breathing.
   (b) Spirometry can be used to measure the extent of recovery of lung function after treatment.
3. (a) Tidal volume vol: 0.5 dm^3
   (b) Expiratory reserve volume vol: 1.0 dm^3
   (c) Residual volume vol: 1.2 dm^3
   (d) Inspiratory capacity vol: 3.8 dm^3
   (e) Vital capacity vol: 4.8 dm^3
   (f) Total lung capacity vol: 6.0 dm^3
4. G: Tidal volume is increasing as a result of exercise.
5. PV: $15 \times 0.4 = 6\ dm^3$
6. (a) During strenuous exercise, PV increases markedly.
   (b) Increased PV is achieved as a result of an increase in both breathing rate and tidal volume.
7. (a) There is 90X more CO_2 in exhaled air than in inhaled air ($3.6 \div 0.04$).
   (b) The CO_2 is the product of cellular respiration in the tissues. Note: Some texts give a value of 4.0% for exhaled air (100X the CO_2 content of inhaled air).
   (c) The dead space air is not involved in gas exchange therefore retains a higher oxygen content than the air that leaves the alveoli. This raises the oxygen content of the expired air.

Review of Lung Function (page 95)

1. (a) Nasal cavity
   (b) Oral cavity
   (c) Trachea
   (e) Terminal bronchiole
   (f) Alveoli
   (i) Medullary respiratory centre
   (ii) Inspiration
   (iii) Expiration
   (iv) Internal intercostal muscles
   (v) External intercostal muscles
   (vi) Ribcage
   (vii) Diaphragm
2. A = Inspiratory reserve volume vol: 3.3 dm^3
   B = Inspiratory capacity vol: 3.8 dm^3
   C = Tidal volume vol: 0.5 dm^3
   D = Expiratory reserve volume vol: 1.0 dm^3
   E = Residual volume vol: 1.2 dm^3

KEY TERMS: Mix and Match (page 96)

Alveoli (V), Breathing (Y), Breathing rate (S), Bronchi (U), Bronchioles (M), Carbon dioxide (N), Cartilage (P), Cellular respiration (Z), Diaphragm (A), Expiration (B), Fick's law (F), Gas exchange surface (E), Gas exchange system (Q), Goblet cells (C), Inspiration (W), Intercostal muscles (I), Lungs (T), Oxygen (G), Pulmonary ventilation rate (X), Spirometry (H), Surfactant (D), Surface area: volume ratio (L), Tidal volume (O), Trachea (R), Ventilation (J), Vital capacity (K).

Transport and Exchange Systems (page 98)

1. As body mass increases, the SA:V ratio decreases. As this occurs diffusion becomes too inefficient and slow to provide raw materials quickly enough to all the cells of larger animals. Mass transport systems are required to transport materials to and from where they are needed.

2. (a) In vertebrates mass transport is used to transport materials around the body.
   (b) Mass transport systems allow materials to be moved over a long distance in complex multicellular organisms. In contrast, small organisms such as the flatworm or single celled eukaryotes have a surface area to volume ratio large enough to allow for materials to be efficiently transported by diffusion.
   (c) The **tissues** and either the **gills** or **lungs** (depending upon the animal).

Open Circulatory Systems (page 99)

1. Fluids are cycled through a heart into the body cavity where they bathe the tissues before moving back to the heart. Hemolymph moves along a dorsal blood vessel to a tubular heart where it is pumped through short vessels to the rest of the body. Hemolymph is assisted to move through the body by muscle movements and re-enters the vessel system through ostia.

2. Because the hemolymph is not contained in vessels it is not under pressure like in a closed circulatory system. As a result hemolymph only oozes slowly through splits in the cuticle.

3. Crustaceans have an advanced vessel system to the point where it is better described as incompletely closed. Insects have a relatively rudimentary vessel system and is much more open than crustaceans.

4. (a) The vessels open into the body cavity and mix with the tissue fluids.
   (b) There are many branched vessels in crustaceans that take hemolymph through the body. It mixes with tissue fluid for only a short time before draining into sinuses and reentering the vessel system.

Closed Circulatory Systems (page 100)

1. Unlike closed systems, open circulatory systems do not have a complete circuit of vessels for blood to pass through from the heart to the body and back again.

2. (a) Blood passes from the gills to the body.
   (b) Blood flows through the systemic circulation at low pressure.

3. (a) Blood returns to the heart after the lungs.
   (b) Blood flows through the systemic circulation at higher pressure than in the single circuit system.

4. By passing blood back to the heart from the lungs, the double circuit system is able to maintain high blood pressure throughout the body. Higher systemic pressures are important for efficient oxygen delivery and processes like renal filtration (which is less important in fish, which use the gills for excretion).

5. (a) The fish heart is a single pump. Blood flows from the atrium to the ventricle.
   (b) The mammalian heart is a double pump with two atria and two ventricles separated by a muscular septum. One pump sends blood to the lungs, the other sends blood to the body.

6. Blood flow within vessels can be regulated by the contraction or relaxing of blood vessel walls. This enables animals to restrict blood flow in some areas and increase it in others in response to need.

The Human Circulatory System (page 102)

1. (a) Head (b) Lungs (c) Liver (d) Gut (intestines) (e) Kidneys (f) Genitals/lower body

The Human Heart (page 103)

1. (a) Pulmonary artery (b) Vena cava (c) Right atrium (d) Right ventricle (e) Aorta (f) Pulmonary vein (g) Left atrium (h) Left ventricle

Positions of heart valves

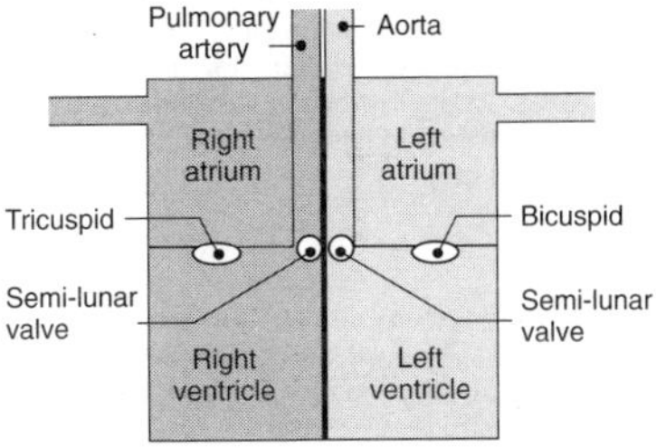

2. **Valves** prevent the blood from flowing the wrong way through the heart and help regulate filling of the heart's chambers.

3. (a) The heart has its own coronary blood supply to meet the high oxygen demands of the heart tissue.
   (b) There must be a system within the heart muscle itself to return deoxygenated blood and waste products of metabolism back to the right atrium.

4. If blood flow to a particular part of the heart is restricted or blocked (because of blocked blood vessel), the part of the heart muscle supplied by that vessel will die, leading to a heart attack or infarction.

5. A: arterioles B: venules C: arterioles D: capillaries

6. (a) The pulse pressure is the difference between the systolic pressure and the diastolic pressure.

(b) Pulse pressure between the aorta and the capillaries will decrease (because of the increasing resistance met on route).

7. (a) You are recording expansion and recoil of the artery that occurs with each contraction of the left ventricle.
   (b) The best place to take a pulse is from the brachial or carotid artery. The blood flow from these arteries (close to the heart) is at a high pressure and still carries the beat or pulse.

Control of Heart Activity (page 105)

1. (a) **Sinoatrial node**: Initiates the cardiac cycle through the spontaneous generation of action potentials.
   (b) **Atrioventricular node**: Delays the impulse.
   (c) **Bundle of His**: Distributes the action potentials over the ventricles (resulting in ventricular contraction).
   (d) **Intercalated discs**: Electrical junctions that allow the action potentials to spread rapidly through the heart muscle without synaptic delay.

2. (a) The heart muscle is capable of rhythmic contraction independently of any external nervous stimulation.
   (b) When the heart is removed from its nervous supply (if provided with adequate oxygen, ions, and fluids) will continue to beat.

3. Delaying the impulse at the AVN allows time for atrial contraction to finish before the ventricles contract.

The Cardiac Cycle (page 106)

1. (a) QRS complex (b) T (c) P

2. During the period of electrical recovery the heart muscle cannot contract. This ensures that the heart has an enforced rest and will not fatigue, nor accumulate lactic acid (as occurs in working skeletal muscle).
3. Extra text removed and letter answers have been placed for each cycle.

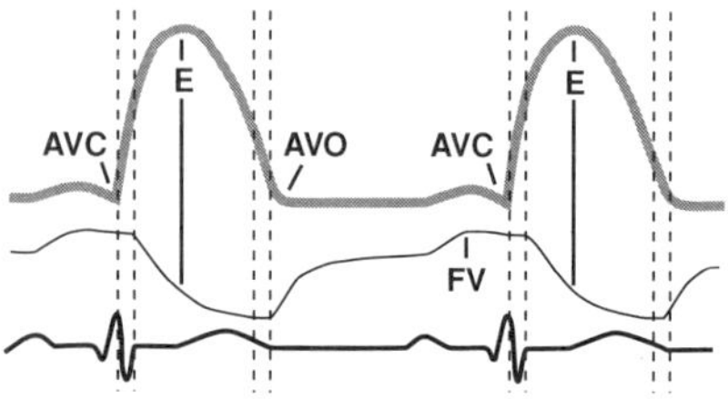

Review of the Human Heart (page 107)

1. (1) Anterior vena cava
   (2) Right atrium
   (3) Sinoatrial node (SAN)
   (4) Atrioventricular node (AVN)
   (5) Bundle of His (atrioventricular bundle)
   (6) Right ventricle
   (7) Left common carotid
   (8) Left subclavian artery
   (9) Aorta
   (10) Pulmonary artery
   (11) Left atrium
   (12) Purkyne fibres
   (13) Left ventricle

2. A = Contraction of the atria.
   B = Contraction of the ventricles.
   C = Relaxation and recovery of ventricles.

3. Use of an artificial pacemaker to regulate heart rhythm.

Arteries (page 108)

1. (a) Tunica externa (c) Endothelium
   (b) Tunica media (d) Blood (or lumen)

2. (a) Thick, elastic walls can withstand the high pressure of the blood being pumped from the heart. **Note**: Elasticity also helps to even out the surges that occur with each contraction of the heart. This keeps the blood moving forward in a continuous flow.
   (b) Blood pressure is low within the arterioles.

3. The smooth muscle around arteries helps to regulate blood flow and pressure. By contracting or relaxing it alters the diameter of the artery and adjusts the volume of blood as required.

4. (a) The diameter of the artery increases.
   (b) The blood pressure decreases.

Veins (page 109)

1. (a) Veins have less elastic and muscle tissue than arteries.
   (b) Veins have a larger lumen than arteries.

2. Most of the structural differences between arteries and veins are related to the different blood pressures inside the vessels. Blood in veins travels at low pressure and veins do not need to be as strong, hence the thinner layers of muscle and elastic tissue and the relatively larger lumen. **Note**: There is still enough elastic and muscle tissue to enable the veins to adjust to changes in blood volume and pressure.

3. Veins are massaged by the skeletal muscles (e.g. leg muscles). Valves (with these muscular movements) help to return venous blood to the heart by preventing backflow away from the heart. **Note**: When skeletal muscles contract and tighten around a vein the valves open and blood is driven towards the heart. When the muscles relax, the valves close, preventing backflow.

4. Venous blood oozes out in an even flow from a wound because it has lost a lot of pressure after passing through the narrow capillary vessels (with their high resistance to flow). Arterial blood spurts out rapidly because it is being pumped directly from the heart and has not yet entered the capillary networks.

Capillaries (page 110)

1. **Capillaries** are very small blood vessels forming networks or beds that penetrate all parts of the body. The only tissue present is an endothelium of squamous epithelial cells. **Arteries** have a thin endothelium, a central layer of elastic tissue and smooth muscle and a thick outer layer of elastic and connective tissue. **Veins** have a thin endothelium, a central layer of elastic and muscle tissue and a thin outer layer of elastic connective tissue. In addition, veins also have valves.

2. (a) Sinusoids differ from capillaries in that they are wider and follow a more convoluted path through

the tissue. They are lined with phagocytic cells rather than the usual endothelial lining of capillaries.
(b) Capillaries and sinusoids are similar in that they both transport blood from arterioles to venules.

Capillary Networks (page 111)

1. Capillaries are branching networks of fine blood vessels where exchanges between blood and tissue take place. Blood enters the network at the arteriolar end and is collected by venues at the venous end. The true capillaries form a network outside of the vascular shunt.

2. The smooth muscle sphincters regulate the blood flow to the capillary network by contracting to restrict blood flow to the network and relaxing to allow blood to flow in. The vascular shunt connects the arteriole and venule and allows blood to bypass the capillaries when the smooth muscle sphincters are contracted.

3 (a) Situation A would occur when the body is restricting blood flow to the capillaries, for example when trying to conserve heat by diverting blood away from the extremities.
(b) Situation B would occur when the body is trying to remove excess heat by diverting blood to the skin and extremities or when the body is trying to provide extra blood to areas of high metabolism, e.g. when exercising or digesting food.

4. A portal venous system drains blood from one capillary network into another. An example is the hepatic portal system which drains blood from the capillary network in the gut lumen to the capillary network in the liver. Normally capillary networks drain into veins that return directly to the heart.

Formation of Tissue Fluid (page 112)

1. Tissue fluid bathes the tissues, providing oxygen and nutrients as well as a medium for the transport (away) of metabolic wastes, e.g. CO_2.

2. Capillary walls are thin enough (endothelium is only one cell thick) to allow substances to move easily in and out by diffusion.

3. (a) Arteriolar end: Hydrostatic pressure predominates in causing fluid to move out of the capillaries.
(b) Venous end: Increased concentration of solutes and reduction in hydrostatic pressure at the venous end of a capillary bed **lowers the solute potential** within the capillary and there is a tendency for water and solutes to re-enter the capillary.

4. (a) Most tissue fluid finds it way directly back into the capillaries as a result of net inward pressure at the venule end of the capillary bed.
(b) The lymph vessels (which parallel the blood system) drain tissue fluid (as lymph) back into the heart, thereby returning it into the main circulation.

Blood (page 113)

1. **Note**: In some cases, the answers below provide more detail than expected. This is provided as extension.
(b) Protection against disease:
Blood component: White blood cells
Mode of action: Engulf bacteria, mediate immune reactions, and allergic and inflammatory responses.
(c) Communication between cells, tissues and organs:
Blood component: Hormones
Mode of action: Specific chemicals which are carried in the blood to target tissues, where they interact with specific receptors and bring about an appropriate response.
(d) Oxygen transport:
Blood component: Haemoglobin molecule of erythrocytes.
Mode of action: Binds oxygen at the lungs and releases it at the tissues.
(e) Carbon dioxide transport:
Blood components: Mainly plasma (most carbon dioxide is carried as bicarbonate in the plasma, a small amount is dissolved in the plasma). Red blood cells (a small amount (10-20%) of carbon dioxide is carried bound to haemoglobin).
Mode of action: Diffuses between tissues, plasma, and lungs according to concentration gradient.
(f) Buffer against pH changes:
Blood components: Haemoglobin molecule of erythrocytes. Plasma bicarbonate and proteins.
Mode of action: Free hydrogen ions are picked up and carried by the haemoglobin molecule (removed from solution). Plasma bicarbonate can form either carbonic acid by picking up a hydrogen ion (H^+), or sodium bicarbonate by combining with sodium ions. Negatively charged proteins also associate with H^+.
(g) Nutrient supply:
Blood component: Plasma
Mode of action: Glucose is carried in the plasma and is taken up by cells (made available throughout the body to all tissues).
(h) Tissue repair:
Blood components: Platelets and leucocytes
Mode of action: Platelets initiate the cascade of reactions involved in clotting and wound repair. Leucocytes (some types) engulf bacteria and foreign material, preventing or halting infection.
(i) Transport of hormones, lipids, and fat soluble vitamins:
Blood component: α-globulins
Mode of action: α-globulins bind these substances and carry them in the plasma. This prevents them being filtered in the kidneys and lost in the urine.

2. Any of: Presence (WBC) or absence (RBC) of **nucleus**. Colour, reflecting presence (RBC) or absence (WBC) of respiratory pigment, **haemoglobin**. **Shape and size** (smaller, dish shaped RBCs vs larger, rounded WBCs. **Mitochondria** present in WBCs, absent in RBCs.

3. (a) Lack of a nucleus allows more space inside the cell to carry Hb (hence greater O_2 carrying capacity).
(b) Lack of mitochondria forces the red blood cells to metabolise anaerobically so that they do not consume the oxygen they are carrying.

4. (a) Elevated eosinophil count: Allergic response such as hay fever or asthma.
(b) Elevated neutrophil count: Microbial infection.
(c) Elevated basophil count: Inflammatory response e.g. as a result of an allergy or a parasitic (as opposed to bacterial) infection.
(d) Elevated lymphocyte count: Infection or response to vaccination.

Gas Transport in Humans (page 115)

1. (a) Oxygen is high in the lung alveoli and in the capillaries leaving the lung.
   (b) Carbon dioxide is high in the capillaries leaving the tissues and in the cells of the body tissues.

2. Haemoglobin binds oxygen reversibly, taking up oxygen when oxygen tensions are high (lungs), carries oxygen to where it is required (the tissues) and releases it.

3. (a) As oxygen level in the blood increases, more oxygen combines with haemoglobin. However, the relationship is not linear: Hb saturation remains high across a wide range of partial pressures of oxygen.
   (b) When oxygen level (partial pressure) in the blood or tissues is very low, haemoglobin saturation declines markedly and oxygen is released (to the tissues).

4. (a) Fetal Hb has a higher affinity for oxygen than adult Hb (it can carry 20-30% more oxygen).
   (b) This higher affinity is necessary because it enables oxygen to pass from the maternal Hb to the foetal Hb across the placenta.

5. (a) The Bohr effect
   (b) Actively respiring tissue consumes a lot of oxygen and generates a lot of CO_2. This lowers tissue (blood) pH causing more oxygen to be released from the haemoglobin to where it is required.

6. Myoglobin preferentially picks up oxygen from Hb and is able to act as an oxygen store in the muscle.

7. Any two of: **Blood proteins**, **haemoglobin**, which picks up H^+ generated by the dissociation of carbonic acid. **Bicarbonate** alone (from this dissociation), and combined with Na^+ (from the dissociation of NaCl).

Transport in Plants (page 120)

1. (a) **Leaves**: Collect the sun's energy and convert it to usable energy (sugar). Control the entry and exit of gases and water vapour (therefore have a role in cooling the plant).
   Roots: Anchor the plant. Absorb water and dissolved minerals. Sometimes store food. Produce new tissue at meristems.
   Stems: Link the roots to the leaves. Provide support for the leaves, fruits, and flowers. Conduct water and dissolved minerals and foods around the plant. Produce new tissue at meristems.
   (b) Materials transported: Water, minerals (e.g. nitrogen, phosphorus), sugar, essential ions (e.g. K^+, Na^+).
   (c) Functions of specific transport tissues:
   Xylem: Transports water and dissolved minerals, plant support. **Phloem**: Transports primarily sugar (in solution), but also minerals, hormones, and amino acids, plant support.

2. Water

3. (a) Xylem: Osmosis (passive movement of water across a partially permeable membrane from less negative to more negative water potential). Also cohesion and root pressure.
   (b) Phloem: Active transport to load the sugar into the phloem tissue, osmosis (water follows sugar into the phloem), pressure-flow of the sap along the phloem.

Stems and Roots (page 121)

1. A: Epidermis
   B: Fibre cap
   C: Phloem
   D: Cortex
   E: Vascular cambium
   F: Xylem
   G: Pith
2. Stems are distinguished by the presence of nodes and internodes.

3. Either of the following:
   - Dicot stems have a large central pith composed of parenchyma cells.
   - The vascular bundles are arranged in an orderly fashion around the periphery of the stem.

4. The cells of the vascular cambium divide to produce the thickening of the stem.

5. Any three of the following:
   - Roots anchor the plant into the soil
   - Absorb water and inorganic nutrients from the soil.
   - Sites for production of hormones gibberellins and cytokinins, which influence growth and development.
   - Specialised roots can have a variety of roles including supporting stems (prop roots), or supplying oxygen to underwater roots (pneumatophores) in the case of mangroves.

6. (a) and (b), any two of:
   - The primary xylem forms a star shape in the root centre (with usually 3 or 4 points).
   - The vascular tissue forms a central cylinder through the root (stele).
   - The stele is surrounded by a pericycle.

7. The parenchyma (packing) cells store starch and other substances.

8. **Root hairs** increase the surface area for absorption.

9. Cap of cells protects the dividing cells behind the root cap, which are delicate and are easily damaged. The cap of cells also has a role in lubricating the root tip and facilitating root movement through the soil.

Leaf Structure (page 123)

1. (a) and (b), any two of the following:
   Hairs on the surface to reduce water loss, waxy cuticle to reduce water loss, sunken stoma to reduce water loss, modified leaves to store water (e.g. succulents), modification of leaves into tendrils to provide climbing support (e.g. pea plant), leaves are modified into spines for defence (e.g. cacti), leave are modified in carnivorous plants to catch prey.

2. The mesophyll is the main location for chloroplasts.

3. Air spaces in the leaf tissue increase the surface area for rapid exchange of gases (CO_2 in and oxygen out).

4. (a) Gas exchange occurs through small pores on the leaf surface called stomata. Carbon dioxide enters and oxygen and water exit.
   (b) Gas exchange is regulated by guard cells which surround each stoma. When the guard cell is turgid the stoma opens. When water moves out of the guard cells, they become flaccid, and the stoma closes, preventing further exchange and water loss.

Xylem (page 124)

1. **Xylem** conducts water and dissolved minerals around the plant (from roots to leaves).
2. (a) Vessel elements: Provide rapid, low resistance conduction of water.
   (b) Tracheids: Role in water conduction but there is more impedance to water flow than in vessels.
   (c) Fibres (and sclereids): Provide mechanical support to the xylem.
   (d) Xylem parenchyma: Involved in storage.
3. Strengthened by having hard fibre cells and sclereids, and spiral thickening of the vessel walls.
4. As well as having pits in the walls (which tracheids also have) the end walls of vessels are perforated.

Phloem (page 125)

1. Phloem conducts dissolved sugar around the plant from its place of production to where it is required.
2. Xylem is dead, phloem is alive. Xylem transports water and minerals, phloem transports dissolved sugar.
3. Perforations enable the sugar solution to pass through and along the sieve tubes.
4. (a) The sieve cell or sieve tube member.
   (b) The companion cell keeps the sieve tube cell alive and controls its activity. They are responsible for loading and unloading sugar into the sieve cells.
5. Phloem parenchyma cells are involved in storage.
6. Strengthening: Fibres and sclereids.

Uptake in the Root (page 126)

1. (a) Passive absorption of minerals along with the water and active transport.
   (b) Apoplastic pathway (about 90%): Moving through the xylem tubes and spaces within the cell walls. Symplastic pathway: Moving through the cell cytoplasm from cell to cell via plasmodesmata.
2. Large water uptake allows plants to take up sufficient quantities of minerals from the soil. These are often in very low concentration in the soil and low water uptakes would not provide adequate quantities.
3. (a) The Casparian strip represents a waterproof barrier to water flow through the apoplastic pathway into the stele. It forces the water to move into the cells (i.e. move via the symplastic route).
   (b) This feature enables the plant to better regulate its uptake of ions, i.e. take up ions selectively. The movement of ions through the apoplast cannot be regulated because the flow does not occur across any partially permeable membranes.

Transpiration (page 127)

1. (a) They take up water by the roots.
   (b) Any of:
   - Transpiration stream enables plants to absorb sufficient quantities of the minerals they need (the minerals are absorbed with the water and are often in low concentration in the soil).
   - Transpiration helps cool the plant.
2. Water moves by osmosis in all cases. In any order:
   (a) **Transpiration pull**: Photosynthesis and evaporative loss of water from leaf surfaces create a more negative water potential in the leaf cells than elsewhere in the plant, facilitating movement of water along a gradient in water potential towards the site of evaporation (stomata).
   (b) **Capillary effect/cohesion-adhesion**: Water molecules cling together and adhere to the xylem, creating an unbroken water column through the plant. The upward pull on the sap creates a tension that facilitates movement of water up the plant.
   (c) **Root pressure** provides a weak push effect for upward water movement.
3. (a)-(c) any of the following: High wind, high light, high temperature, low humidity. All increase the rate of evaporation from the leaves.
4. The system excludes air. As the plant loses water through transpiration, it takes up water from the flask via roots (or cut stem). The volume removed from the flask by the plant is withdrawn from the pipette; this can be measured on the pipette graduations.
5. (a) Measurements were taken at the start and at the end of the experiment in the same conditions (still air, light shade, 20°C). These rates should be the same (give or take experimental error). This indicates that the plant has not been damaged by the experiment and any results are therefore a real response to the experimental conditions.
   (b) Moving air and bright sunlight increase transpiration rate, because they increase the rate of evaporation from the leaves. **Note**: Lower humidity could also be said to increase transpiration rate (by increasing the gradient in water potential), but this would need to be tested further, i.e. the results here do not conclusively show this. Another test where the effects of darkness and humidity level were separated would be required. This is a good discussion point for students investigating experimental design and interpretation of results.
   (c) Still, humid conditions reduce evaporative loss, dark conditions stop photosynthetic production of sugars (therefore solute concentration in the leaves falls). Both these reduce transpiration rate by reducing the concentration gradient for water movement.

Adaptations of Xerophytes (page 129)

1. Xeromorphic adaptations allow xerophytes to survive and grow in areas with low or irregular water supplies.
2. (a)-(c), three in any order:
   - Modification of leaves to reduce transpirational loss (e.g. spines, curling, leaf hairs).
   - Shallow, but extensive fibrous root system to extend area from which water is taken and to take advantage of overnight condensation.
   - Water storage in stems or leaves.
   - Rounded, squat shape of plant body to reduce surface area for water loss.
3. The CAM metabolism (found only in xerophytic plants, many of which are succulents) allows carbon dioxide to be fixed during the dark. This produces organic acids which accumulate in the leaves and later release carbon dioxide into the Calvin cycle during daylight

(when light energy is available to provide H^+ and ATP for photosynthesis). The stomata can then stay closed during the day when transpirational losses are highest.

4. A moist microenvironment reduces the gradient in water potential between the leaf and the air, so there is less tendency for water to leave the plant.

5. In a high salt environment, free water is scarce. Sea shoreline plants (halophytes) therefore have many xerophytic adaptations.

Translocation (page 131)

1. (a) '**Source to sink**' means the sugar flows from its site of production (in the leaves) to its site of unloading (at the roots).
   (b) Usual source: Leaves and sometimes stems. Usual sink: Roots.
   (c) Other source: Tubers or other storage organs from which sugar may be mobilised when photosynthetic tissues are absent.
   (d) Other sink: Fruits where sugar is required to form the succulent tissues of the fruit.

2. The energy is required to generate the gradient in H^+ that is used to drive the transport of sucrose into the transfer cell.

3. (a) Translocation: The transport (around the plant) of the organic products of photosynthesis.
   (b) The bulk movement of phloem sap along a gradient in hydrostatic pressure (generated osmotically).
   (c) The coupling of sucrose transport (into the transfer cell) to the diffusion of H^+ down a concentration gradient (generated by a proton pump).

4. The increase in dissolved sugar in the sieve tube cell decreases its water potential. Because of this, water moves into the sieve tube cells by osmosis (water moves to regions of lower water potential).

5. The transfer cell uses active transport mechanisms (coupled transport of sucrose) to accumulate sucrose to levels 2-3 times those in the mesophyll. The sucrose then moves into the sieve tube cell.

6. Xylem sap is only water and dissolved minerals; phloem sap is a 30% sugar (mainly sucrose) solution.

7. Transport of sugars in phloem is active and requires energy expenditure. For this, the tissue must be alive. Movement of water in xylem is a passive process.

8. If sap moved by pressure-flow, then there should be selective pressure for the sieve plate to be lost or become less of a barrier, yet this has not happened. (Of course, there are also selective pressures that operate against loss of the sieve plate, e.g. the need to have discrete yet freely communicating cells).

KEY TERMS: Mix and Match (page 133)

Apoplastic pathway (N), Bulk flow (O), Capilary action (L), Casparian strip (Y), Cohesion-tension hypothesis (M), Companion cells (I), Cortex (D), Endodermis (P), Guard cells (J), Mass flow hypothesis (E), Osmosis (C), Phloem (Q), Root hair (X), Root pressure (W), Sieve tube cells (H), Sink (A), Source (S), Stomata (K), Symplastic pathway (T), Translocation (R), Transpiration (Z), Transpiration pull (U), Turgor (V), Vessel (B), Water potential (F), Xylem (G)

The Biochemical Nature of the Cell (page 136)

1. (a) Lipids are important as a ready store of concentrated energy (their energy yield per gram is twice that of carbohydrates). They also provide insulation and a medium in which to transport fat-soluble vitamins. Phospholipids are a major component of cellular membranes.
   (b) Carbohydrates are a major component of most plant cells, a ready source of energy, and they are involved in cellular recognition. They can also be changed into fats.
   (c) Proteins are required for growth and repair of cells. They may be structural, catalytic, or have a variety of other functions as well as being able to be converted into fats.
   (d) Nucleic acids, e.g. DNA and RNA, encode the genetic information for the construction and functioning of an organism.

2. Inorganic molecules are formally defined with reference to what they are not, i.e. organic. They are important in the structure and metabolism of living things as part of biological molecules, as cofactors (e.g. Mg^{2+}), in redox reactions (e.g. Fe^{2+}), and as a component of intra-and extracellular fluids (e.g. K^+, Na^+). Organic molecules are those containing carbon, with the exception of elemental carbon and a few types of carbon-containing inorganic compounds such as carbonates, and cyanides. Organic molecules make up the biological molecules that form organisms: carbohydrates, nucleic acids, proteins, and lipids.

The Role of Water (page 137)

1.

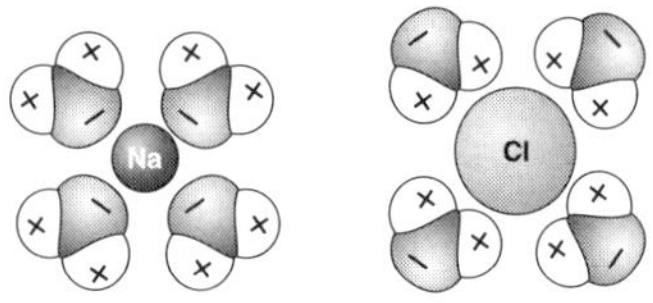

Water surrounding a positive ion (Na^+) — Water surrounding a negative ion (Cl^-)

2. The **dipole nature** of water means that it is a good solvent for many substances, e.g. ionic solids and other polar molecules such as sugars and amino acids. It is therefore readily involved in biochemical reactions.

3. (a) Clarity: Property: Water is colourless and light penetrates through it. Biological importance: This property allows photosynthesis to continue to considerable depth. The photosynthetic region (the euphotic zone) supports life on Earth.
   (b) Xylem transport: Property: Cohesive properties and high tensile strength. Biological importance: These properties allow water molecules to stick together and move cohesively through vessels to considerable heights (important in water and mineral uptake from the soil).
   (c) Thermal stability: Property: High specific heat capacity; water absorbs large amounts of energy for a small rise in temperature. Biological importance: The thermal stability of aquatic environments allows organisms (without thermoregulatory abilities) to maintain stable internal temperatures despite

fluctuations in seasonal air temperatures.

(d) Glucose transport: Property: Water is the universal solvent. Biological importance: Solvent properties of water enable materials such as glucose to be transported around the body.

(e) Cooling effect of evaporation: Property: High latent heat of vaporisation; water absorbs large amounts of energy before evaporating. Biological importance: Organisms in fluctuating environments use sweating and transpiration effectively in temperature control.

(f) Ice floating: Ice is less dense than water. Biological importance: Ice floats so organisms can live underneath it and insulates the underlying water.

Organic Molecules (page 138)

1. Carbon, hydrogen, and oxygen.
2. Sulfur and nitrogen.
3. Four covalent bonds (valency of 4).
4. A molecular (or chemical) formula shows the numbers and kinds of atoms in a molecule whereas a structural formula is the graphical representation of the molecular structure showing how the atoms are arranged.
5. A functional group is an atom or group of atoms, such as a carboxyl group, that replaces hydrogen in an organic compound and that defines the structure of a family of compounds and determines the properties of the family.
6. It is an aldehyde.
7. Amine group (NH_2) or carboxyl group (COOH).
8. The amino acid cysteine has an R group (SH) that can form disulfide bridges with other cysteines to create cross linkages in a polypeptide chain (protein).

Amino Acids (page 139)

1. They are the building blocks for constructing proteins (which have diverse structural and metabolic functions). Amino acids are also the precursors of many important molecules (e.g. neurotransmitters and hormones).
2. The side chains (R groups) differ in their chemical structure (and therefore their chemical effect).
3. Translation of the genetic code. Genetic instructions from the chromosomes (genes on the DNA) determine the order in which amino acids are joined together.
4. **Essential amino acids** cannot be manufactured by the human body, they must be included in the food we eat.
5. **Condensation reactions** involve the joining of two amino acids (or an amino acid to a dipeptide or polypeptide) by a peptide bond with the release of a water molecule.
6. **Hydrolysis** involves the splitting of a dipeptide (or the splitting of an amino acid from a polypeptide) where the peptide bond is broken and a water molecule is used to provide a hydrogen atom and a hydroxyl group.
7. The L-form.

Proteins (page 141)

1. (a) **Structural**: Proteins form an important component of connective tissues and epidermal structures: collagen, keratin (hair, horn etc.). Proteins are also found scattered on, in, and through cell membranes, but tend to have a regulatory role in this instance. Proteins are also important in maintaining a tightly coiled structure in a condensed chromosome.

   (b) **Regulatory**: **Hormones** such as insulin, adrenaline (modified amino acid), glucagon (peptide) are chemical messengers released from glands to trigger a response in a target tissue. They help maintain homeostasis. **Enzymes** regulate metabolic processes in cells.

   (c) **Contractile**: Actin and myosin are structural components of muscle fibres. Using a ratchet system, these two proteins move past each other when energy is supplied.

   (d) **Immunological**: Gamma globulins are blood proteins that act as antibodies, targeting antigens (foreign substances and microbes) for immobilisation and destruction.

   (e) **Transport**: Haemoglobin and myoglobin are proteins that act as carrier molecules for transporting oxygen in the bloodstream of vertebrates. Invertebrates usually have some other type of oxygen carrying molecule in the blood.

   (f) **Catalytic**: Enzymes, e.g. amylase, lipase, lactase, trypsin, are involved in the chemical digestion of food. A vast variety of other enzymes are involved in just about every metabolic process in organisms.

2. Denaturation destroys protein function because it involves an irreversible change in the precise tertiary or quaternary structure that confers biological activity. For example, a denatured enzyme protein may not have its reactive sites properly aligned, and will be prevented from attracting the substrate molecule.

3. Any one of:
   - Globular proteins have a tertiary structure that produces a globular or spherical shape. Fibrous proteins have a tertiary structure that produces long chains or sheets, often with many cross-linkages.
   - The structure of fibrous proteins makes them insoluble in water. The spherical nature of globular proteins makes them water soluble.

4. (a) 21 amino acids (b) 29 amino acids

Modification of Proteins (page 143)

1. (a) **Glycoproteins** are proteins with attached carbohydrates (often relatively small polymers of sugar units).

   (b) In any order, three roles of glycoproteins:
   - **Intercellular recognition**: Present on cell surfaces for recognition between cells (when cells interact to form tissues and for immune function).
   - **Transport**: Embedded in cell membranes to transport molecules through the membrane (the sugars help to maintain the position of the glycoprotein in the membrane).
   - **Regulation**: Secretory proteins from glands with a role in regulation, e.g. many pituitary hormones.

2. (a) **Lipoproteins** are proteins with attached fatty acid molecules.

   (b) Lipoproteins transport lipid molecules in the plasma between different organs in the body.

3. Proteins made on free ribosomes are released directly into the cytoplasm; there is no facility for attachment of carbohydrate as this generally requires a packaging region (the Golgi apparatus).

4. Protein orientation in the membrane is important because it is usually critical to the functional role of the protein, e.g. in intercellular recognition or transport.

Monosaccharides and Disaccharides (page 144)

1. (a) Primary energy source for cellular metabolism
   (b) Structural units for disaccharides and polysaccharides (energy sources and structural carbohydrates).

2. (a) Lactose
   Enzyme: lactase
   Products: glucose and galactose
   Found: In the small intestine of mammals (secreted by the intestinal epithelial cells)
   (b) Maltose
   Enzyme: maltase
   Products: glucose monomers
   Found: In the intestine of animals (secreted by the intestinal epithelial cells), in germinating seeds. It is also found in bacteria and yeasts.
   (c) Sucrose
   Enzyme: sucrase or invertase
   Products: glucose and fructose
   Found: Sucrase is found in the small intestine of mammals (secreted by the intestinal epithelial cells). Invertase is found in plants and yeasts, and is also produced by honeybees. Note invertase and sucrase both hydrolyse sucrose but by different mechanisms: Invertases cleave the O-C(fructose) bond, whereas the sucrases cleave the O-C(glucose) bond

3. A lactose intolerance would arise when a person fails to produce lactase in the small intestine and so cannot metabolise lactose, which passes into the colon uncleaved (bacterial utilisation of this substrate in the colon causes the intestinal symptoms of the intolerance). **Teacher's note**: Lactase production naturally declines in adulthood, but a mutation on chromosome 2 prevents this lactase shutdown and enables utilisation of lactose throughout adult life. This mutation has arisen independently in northern Europe and east Africa and appears to be an evolutionarily recent adaptation to dairy consumption.

Carbohydrate Chemistry (page 145)

1. **Structural isomers** have the same molecular formula but their atoms are linked in different sequences. For example, fructose and glucose are structural isomers because, although they have the same molecular formula ($C_6H_{12}O_6$), glucose contains an aldehyde group (it is an aldose) and fructose contains a keto group (it is a ketose). In contrast, **optical isomers** are identical in every way except that they are mirror images of each other. The two ring forms of glucose, α and β glucose, are optical isomers, being two mirror image forms.

2. Compound sugars are formed and broken down by condensation and hydrolysis reactions respectively. **Condensation reactions** join two carbohydrate molecules by a glycosidic bond with the release of a water molecule. **Hydrolysis reactions** use water to split a carbohydrate molecule into two, where the water molecule is used to provide a hydrogen atom and a hydroxyl group.

3. Isomers will have different bonding properties and will form different disaccharides and macromolecules depending on the isomer involved, e.g. glucose and fructose are structural isomers; glucose + glucose forms maltose, glucose + fructose from sucrose. A polysaccharide of the α isomer of glucose forms starch whereas the β isomer forms cellulose.

Polysaccharides (page 146)

1. Polysaccharides are a good source of energy because they are easily hydrolysed into monosaccharides (e.g. glucose) when energy is needed. Monosaccharides are the primary source of cellular fuel.

2. Cellulose, starch, and glycogen are all polymers of glucose, but differ in form and function because of the optical isomer involved, the length of the polymers, and the degree of branching. **Cellulose** is an unbranched, long chain glucose polymer held by β-1,4 glycosidic bonds. The straight, tightly packed chains give cellulose high tensile strength and resistance to hydrolysis. **Starch** is a mixture of two polysaccharides: amylose (unbranched with α-1,4 glycosidic bonds) and amylopectin (branched with α-1,6 glycosidic bonds). The α-1,4 glycosidic bonds and more branched nature of starch account for its physical properties; starch is powdery and more easily hydrolysed than cellulose, which exists as tough microfibrils. **Glycogen**, like starch, is a branched polymer. It is similar to amylopectin, being composed of α-glucose molecules, but it is larger and more there are more α-1,6 links. This makes it highly branched, more soluble, and more easily hydrolysed than starch.

Cellulose and Starch (page 147)

1. Cellulose is a linear molecule consisting of several hundred to several thousand β-glucose molecules bonded by a 1,4 glycosidic bond. Starch is composed of two main molecules; amylose which forms a helix, and a branched molecule, amylopectin. Amylose consists of α-glucose monomers bonded by 1-4 glycosidic bonds. Amylopectin also consists of α-glucose monomers, but around 4% of its bonds are 1,6 glycosidic bonds, which causes it to branch.

2. Cellulose has a structural role, providing strength and support to the plant cell. Starch provides the plant with a means of storing energy. Glucose molecules are stored as starch inside amyloplasts in a compact form which can be easily hydrolysed to be released as an energy source when required.

3. The lattice structure of the cells in wood provide a low density structure while the cellulose (making up 50% of wood) provides strength.

4. Cellulose microfibrils are composed of molecules that possess strong intramolecular bonds (covalent bonds) as well as having strong hydrogen bonding between cellulose molecules.

5. (a) ~650 MPa (b) ~540 MPa
   (c) ~140 MPa (d) ~ 620 MPa

Lipids (page 149)

1. (a) Saturated fatty acids contain the maximum number of hydrogen atoms, whereas unsaturated fatty acids contain some double-bonded carbon atoms.
   (b) Saturated fatty acids tend to produce lipids that are solid at room temperature, whereas lipids that contain a high proportion of unsaturated fatty acids tend to be liquid at room temperature.

2. (a) Energy: Fats provide a compact, easily stored source of energy. Energy yield per gram on oxidation is twice that of carbohydrate.
   (b) Water: Metabolism of lipids releases water. **Note**: oxidation of triglycerides releases twice as much water as carbohydrate.
   (c) Insulation: Heat does not dissipate easily through fat therefore thick fat insulates against heat loss.

3. In **phospholipids**, one of the fatty acids is replaced with a phosphate; the molecule is ionised and the phosphate end is water soluble. **Triglycerides** are non-polar and not soluble in water.

4. Saturated fats are solid at room temperature because they comprise mostly saturated fatty acids. These contain the maximum number of hydrogen atoms and form straight molecules that pack tightly together.

5. (a) The amphipathic nature of phospholipids causes them to orientate in aqueous solutions so that the hydrophobic 'tails' point in together. Hence the bilayer nature of phospholipid membranes.
   (b) The cellular membranes of an Arctic fish could be expected to contain a higher proportion of unsaturated fatty acids and more cholesterol than those of a tropical fish species. This would help them to remain fluid at low temperatures.

6. Cholesterol is an amphipathic molecule. It contains a hydroxyl (-OH) group as well a steroid ring structure and a hydrocarbon chain. The -OH group can interact with the polar head groups of the membrane phospholipids, stabilising the outer surface of the membrane and making it less permeable to some ions (less leaky). The steroid ring and hydrocarbon chain tuck into the hydrophobic part of the membrane, where the kinked structure increases membrane fluidity (in the same way that unsaturated fatty acids do) by preventing the phospholipids from packing too closely together.

Biochemical Tests (page 151)

1. Lipids are insoluble in water. They will not form an emulsion in water unless they have first been dissolved in ethanol (a non-polar solvent).

2. (a) To quantify the glucose concentration of commercial drinks, you would (1) perform a Benedict's test on each of the unknown drinks (dilute if necessary), (2) measure the absorbance value of the colour change, (3) use the calibration curve prepared from a series of know glucose standards to read off the glucose concentration of the unknowns.
   (b) You would have to dilute the drinks so the concentrations fell within the range of the curve.

3. The acidic conditions break the glycosidic bond in a non-reducing sugar (e.g sucrose) through hydrolysis. The products of decomposition (e.g. of sucrose) are monosaccharides (e.g. glucose and fructose), both of which can be detected by Benedict's reagent.

4. An emulsion is a mixture of two immiscible liquids, and one is dispersed in the other. The mix of properties scatters light and makes the mixture appear cloudy.

KEY TERMS: Word Find (page 152)

G	L	O	B	U	L	A	R	T	V	C	E	L	L	U	L	O	S	E	O	B	F	P	O	S
D	B	I	I	S	D	E	X	E	R	G	O	N	I	C	F	G	Q	E	F	E	H	L	T	D
E	R	R	N	T	A	N	A	B	O	L	I	C	J	R	Y	U	D	L	G	Q	E	A	B	M
N	M	W	Q	X	S	F	E	E	U	R	L	G	L	Y	C	O	G	E	N	V	F	P	O	X
A	J	C	V	U	A	C	O	N	D	E	N	S	A	T	I	O	N	V	S	L	N	Z	Q	L
T	J	S	A	T	U	R	A	T	E	D	P	D	C	O	W	F	Q	W	A	X	O	F	K	B
U	Q	J	H	Y	F	F	I	S	O	M	E	R	S	S	H	Y	D	R	O	L	Y	S	I	S
R	F	O	O	A	G	U	D	I	P	E	P	T	I	D	E	L	T	F	I	B	R	O	U	S
A	Z	F	J	H	C	O	L	O	R	I	M	E	T	R	Y	U	A	J	U	H	F	M	A	N
T	I	N	D	U	C	E	D	F	I	T	G	F	H	N	E	M	O	L	E	C	U	L	A	R
I	Z	L	M	K	S	T	A	R	C	H	P	J	Z	N	Z	L	M	O	S	W	V	G	X	W
O	M	B	R	Y	G	A	L	I	P	I	D	S	X	C	U	D	I	P	O	L	A	R	W	A
N	Q	S	X	B	V	B	K	U	P	U	E	C	P	T	S	Q	C	A	B	O	I	F	N	T
P	R	I	M	A	R	Y	S	T	R	U	C	T	U	R	E	A	V	T	Y	R	U	R	J	E
C	H	I	T	I	N	A	M	I	N	O	A	C	I	D	S	B	G	D	F	C	P	K	O	R
D	H	V	T	T	E	R	T	I	A	R	Y	S	T	R	U	C	T	U	R	E	X	W	C	N
B	V	O	R	G	A	N	I	C	V	S	Z	P	H	O	S	P	H	O	L	I	P	I	D	S

DNA Molecules (page 154)

1. (a) 95 times more base pairs
   (b) 630 times more base pairs

2. < 2% encodes proteins or structural RNA.

3. (a) and (b) in any order:
   (a) Much of the once considered 'junk DNA' has now been found to give rise to functional RNA molecules (many with regulatory functions).
   (b) Complex organisms contain much more of this non-protein-coding DNA which suggests that these sequences contain RNA-only 'hidden' genes that have been conserved through evolution and have a definite role in the development of the organism.

Eukaryote Chromosome Structure (page 155)

1. (a) **DNA**: A long, complex nucleic acid molecule found in the chromosomes of nearly all organisms (some viruses have RNA instead). Provides the genetic instructions (genes) for the production of proteins and other gene products (e.g. RNAs).
   (b) **Chromatin**: Chromosomal material consisting of DNA, RNA, and histone and non-histone proteins. The term is used in reference to chromosomes in the non-condensed state.
   (c) **Histone**: Simple proteins that bind to DNA and help it to coil up during cell division. Histones are also involved in regulating DNA function in some way.
   (d) **Centromere**: A bump or constriction along the length of a chromosome to which spindle fibres attach during cell division. The centromere binds two chromatids together.
   (e) **Chromatid**: One of a pair of duplicated chromosomes produced prior to cell division, joined at the centromere. The terms chromatid and chromosome distinguish duplicated chromosomes before and after division of the centromere.

2. The chromatin (DNA and associated proteins) combine to coil up the DNA into a "super coiled" arrangement. The coiling of the DNA occurs at several levels. The DNA molecule is wrapped around bead-like cores of (8) histone proteins (called nucleosomes), which are separated from each other by linker DNA sequences of about 50 bp. The histones (H1) are responsible for pulling nucleosomes together to form a 30 nm fibre. The chromatin fibre is then folded and wrapped so that it is held in a tight configuration. The different levels of coiling enables a huge amount of DNA to be packed, without tangling, into a very small space in a well organised, orderly fashion.

Nucleic Acids (page 157)

1. (a)-(e) See below (only half of the section of DNA illustrated in the workbook is shown here):

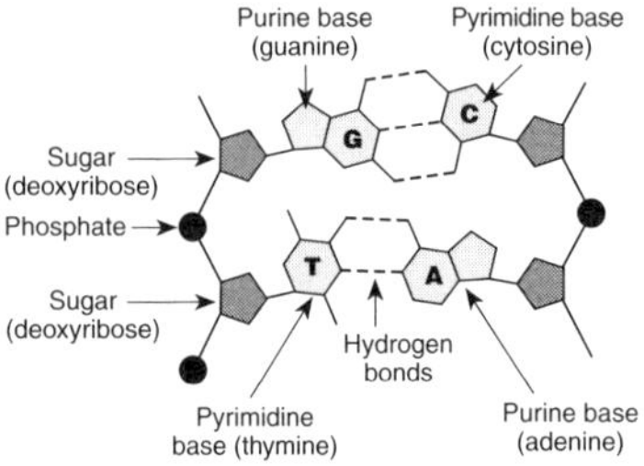

2. (a) The following bases always pair in a normal double strand of DNA: guanine with cytosine, cytosine with guanine, thymine with adenine, adenine with thymine.
   (b) In mRNA, uracil replaces thymine in pairing with adenine.
   (c) The hydrogen bonds in double stranded DNA hold the two DNA strands together.

3. **Nucleotides** are building blocks of nucleic acids (DNA, RNA). Their precise sequence provides the genetic blueprint for the organism.

4. The **template strand** of DNA is complementary to the **coding strand** and provides the template for the transcription of the mRNA molecule. The coding strand has the same nucleotide sequence as the mRNA (it carries the code), except that thymine in the coding strand substitutes for uracil in the mRNA.

5.

	DNA	**RNA**
Sugar present	Deoxyribose	Ribose
Bases present	Adenine	Adenine
	Guanine	Guanine
	Cytosine	Cytosine
	Thymine	Uracil
Number of strands	Two (double)	One (single)
Relative length	Long	Short

Creating a DNA Model (page 159)

3. Labels as follows:

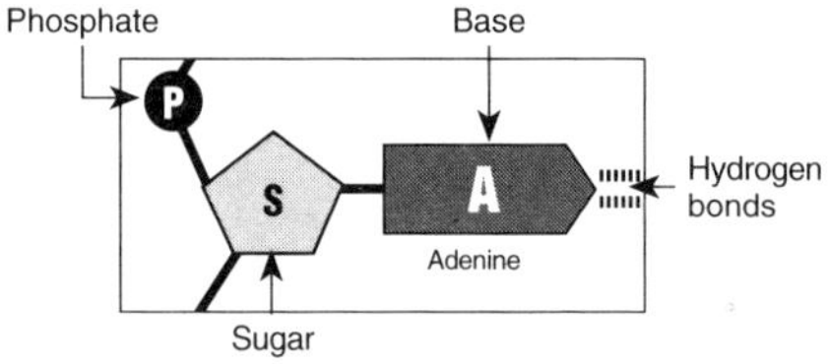

4. & 5.

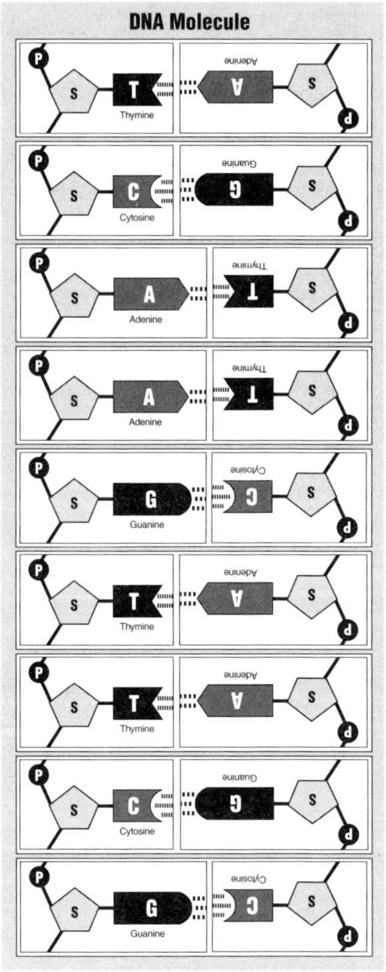

6. Factors that prevent a mismatch of nucleotides:
   - The number of hydrogen bond attraction points
   - The size (length) of the base (thymine and cytosine are short, adenine and guanine are long).

DNA Replication (page 163)

1. DNA replication prepares a chromosome for cell division by producing two chromatids which are (or should be) identical copies of the genetic information for the chromosome.

2. (a) Step 1: Enzymes unwind DNA molecule to expose the two original strands.
   (b) Step 2: DNA polymerase enzyme uses the two original strands as templates to make complementary strands.
   (c) Step 3: The two resulting double-helix molecules coil up to form two chromatids in the chromosome.

3. (a) **Helicase**: Unwinds the 'parental' strands.
   (b) **DNA polymerase I**: Hydrolyses the RNA primer and replaces it with DNA.
   (c) **DNA polymerase III**: Elongates the leading strand. It synthesises the new Okazaki fragment until it encounters the primer on the previous fragment.
   (d) **Ligase**: Joins Okazaki fragments into a continuous length of DNA.

4. 16 minutes 40 seconds
   4 million nucleotides replicated at the rate of 4000 per second: 4 000 000 ÷ 4000 = 1000 s
   Convert to minutes = 1000 ÷ 60 = 16.67 minutes
   (Note that, under ideal conditions, most of a bacteria's cell cycle is spent in cell division).

Review of DNA Replication (page 165)

1. (a) G pairs with C
   A pairs with T
   (b) A: Parent DNA
   B: Swivel point or replication fork
   C: DNA Polymerase III
   D: Parent strand of DNA in the new DNA molecule
   E: Daughter strand of DNA in the new DNA molecule
   F: Free nucleotide

3. Steps 1-4 as follows:
   1: DNA strands are joined by base pairing.
   2: Unwinding of parent DNA double helix.
   3: Unzipping of DNA parent.
   4: Free nucleotides occupy spaces along exposed bases.

Meselson and Stahl's Experiment (page 166)

1. Generation 1 consisted of only intermediate DNA. This ruled out the conservative method where equal quantities of heavy and light DNA would be expected. Generation 2 produced light and intermediate DNA in equal amounts. This ruled out the dispersive method which would produce a single type of DNA that would separate out somewhere between the intermediate and light bands.

2. (a) Conservative (b) Dispersive

The Simplest Case: Genes to Proteins (page 167)

1. This exercise shows the way in which DNA codes for proteins. Nucleotide has no direct protein equivalent.
   (a) Triplet codes for amino acid.
   (b) Gene codes for polypeptide chain (may be a polypeptide, protein, or RNA product).
   (c) Transcription unit codes for functional protein.

2. (a) **Nucleotides** are made up of: Phosphate, sugar, and one of four bases (adenine, guanine, cytosine, and thymine or uracil).
   (b) **Triplet** is made up of three consecutive nucleotide bases that are read together as a code.
   (c) **Gene** comprises a sequence of triplets, starting with a start code and ending with a termination code.
   (d) **Transcription unit** is made up of two or more genes that together code for a functional protein.

3. Extra detail is provided; essential key words in bold. Steps in making a functional protein:
   - The template strand is made from the DNA coding strand and is transcribed into mRNA (**transcription**).
   - The code on the mRNA is translated into a sequence of amino acids (**translation**), which are linked with peptide bonds to form a polypeptide chain (this may be a functional protein in its own right).
   - The proteins coded by two or more genes come together to form the final functional protein (**folding into functional tertiary structure**).

The Genetic Code (page 168)

1. (a) DNA: ATG GGT TAC CTG AGG GTA ATA CGG GCA CTT TAG
   (b) mRNA: AUG GGU UAC CUG AGG GUA AUA CGG GCA CUU UAG
   Amino acids: Met Gly Tyr Leu Arg Val Iso Arg Ala Leu STOP

2. (a) Start: AUG STOP: UAA, UAG, UGA
   (b) They indicate the starting and finishing points on the mRNA (as dictated by the DNA) for the instructions enabling the construction of a polypeptide chain.

Key Terms: Mix and Match (page 169)

Amino acid (J), Antiparallel (Y), Base-pairing rule (P), Codon (V), DNA (Q), DNA ligase (X), DNA polymerase (O), DNA replication (I), Gene expression (C), Genetic code (D), Genome (L), Helicase (K), Histone (A), Hydrogen bonds (B), Lagging strand (G), Leading strand (E), Nucleic acids (U), Nucleotides (R), Okazaki fragments (S), Protein (N), Purine (M), Pyrimidine (W), Replication fork (H), RNA (F), Semi-conservative replication (T).

Enzymes (page 171)

1. The active site is the region where substrate is drawn in and positioned in such a way as to promote the reaction. The properties of the active site are a function of the precise configuration of the amino acid side chains which interact with the substrate.

2. A mutation could result in a different amino acid being positioned in the polypeptide chain. The final protein may be folded incorrectly (incorrect tertiary and quaternary structure) and lose its biological function. **Note**: If the mutation is silent or in a non-critical region of the enzyme, biological function may not be affected.

3. **Catabolism** involves metabolic reactions that break large molecules into smaller ones. Such reactions include digestion and cellular respiration. They release

energy and are therefore **exergonic**. In contrast, **anabolism** involves metabolic reactions that build larger molecules from smaller ones. Anabolic reactions include protein synthesis and photosynthesis. They require the input of energy and are **endergonic**.

How Enzymes Work (page 172)

1. Enzymes are biological molecules (usually proteins) that act as catalysts, allowing reactions to proceed more readily. They do this by influencing bond stability in the reactants and thereby lowering the activation energy required to create an unstable transition state in the substrate from which the reaction proceeds readily.
2. The **lock and key model** proposed that the substrate was simply drawn into a closely matching cleft (active site) on the enzyme. In this model, the enzyme's active site was a somewhat passive recipient of the substrate, whereas studies of enzyme inhibitors since showed that assumption to be incorrect.
3. The **induced fit model** is a modified version of the lock and key in which the substrate and the active site interact. Substrate binding causes the active site to change slightly so that bonds in the substrate(s) are destabilised. This model is supported by evidence from studies of enzyme inhibition.

Enzyme Reaction Rates (page 173)

1. (a) An increase in enzyme concentration increases reaction rate.
   (b) By manufacturing more or less (increasing or decreasing the rate of protein synthesis).
2. (a) An increase in substrate concentration increases reaction rate to a point. Reaction rate then levels off as the amount of substrate continues to increase.
   (b) The reaction rate changes because after a certain substrate level the enzymes are fully saturated by substrate and the rate cannot increase any more.
3. (a) An optimum **temperature** for an enzyme is the temperature at which enzyme activity is maximum.
   (b) Most enzymes perform poorly at low temperatures because chemical reactions occur slowly or not all at low temperatures (enzyme activity will reappear when the temperature increases; usually enzymes are not damaged by moderately low temperatures).
4. (a) Optimum **pH**: Pepsin: 1-2, trypsin: approx. 7.5-8.2, urease: approx. 6.5-7.0
   (b) The stomach is an acidic environment which is the ideal pH for pepsin.

Enzyme Cofactors (page 174)

1. **Cofactors** are non-protein components that complete an enzyme, i.e. enable its functional catalytic activity.
2. Cofactors either complete the active site or make the active site more reactive (e.g. by facilitating the substrate-enzyme interaction).
3. The apoenzyme is the protein portion of the functionally active enzyme. The cofactor is the non-protein portion required to complete the enzyme's catalytic activity.
4. Two broad categories of cofactors are **organic cofactors**, such as vitamin C, and **inorganic ions** (such as Ca^{2+} and Zn^{2+})
5. Many vitamins and minerals are cofactors so an adequate dietary intake ensures that all necessary cofactors are present as required for enzyme function.

Enzyme Inhibitors (page 175)

1. In **competitive inhibition**, the inhibitor competes with the substrate for the enzyme's active site and, once in place, prevents substrate binding. A **noncompetitive inhibitor** does not occupy the active site but binds to some other part of the enzyme, making it less able to perform its function as an effective biological catalyst.
2. (a) With a competitive inhibitor present, the effect of the competition can be overcome by increasing the substrate concentration; the rate of the reaction will slow, but will eventually reach the same level as that achieved without an inhibitor. In a system where there is a non-competitive inhibitor, the rate of the reaction slows and is well below the maximum that can be achieved without an inhibitor. This rate depression cannot be overcome by increasing the substrate concentration.
   (b) Type of inhibition could be tested by increasing the substrate concentration. If this overcame the rate depression then the inhibition is competitive.
3. Noncompetitive inhibition is similar to allosteric inhibition in that they both involve the inhibitor binding at a site other than the active site, thereby changing the conformation of the active site and stopping the activity of the enzyme. However, allosteric inhibition is always reversible and a feature of regulation in metabolic pathways. Non-competitive inhibition may be irreversible, in which case the inhibitor is a poison.
4. Heavy metals are toxic because they permanently stop enzyme activity, rendering the enzyme non-functional usually, but not exclusively, through non-competitive inhibition. Because they are lost exceedingly slowly from the body, anything other than a low level of these metals is toxic.
5. (a) Some antibiotics, such as penicillin, are irreversible inhibitors to the enzymes essential for wall synthesis in bacteria. Susceptible bacteria are unable to build cell walls after dividing so their growth is stopped.
   (b) Human cells do not have a cell wall and so they are unaffected by the enzyme inhibition.

Global Human Nutrition (page 178)

1. In developing countries malnutrition is most commonly associated with undernutrition. Undernutrition describes a situation where the total food intake is not adequate. The range of foods consumed are often limited and deficient in certain nutrients causing malnutrition. In the developed world, the supply of food is plentiful and the amounts consumed often exceed the body's daily requirements. In this instance malnutrition arises from consuming an unbalanced diet which is calorie rich, highly processed, and lacking in nutrients.
2. The modern industrialised agricultural techniques on which global food production is currently based are heavily reliant on fossil fuels, which are used to produce fertilisers and operate machinery. The

decades following peak oil (when oil supplies peak and begins to decline), will see sharp increases in oil prices and consequently a rise in the costs of food production. This will causes food shortages through a number of interconnected mechanisms:

- increased costs of food production will be passed on as increased costs of food to consumers. This will disproportionately disadvantage poor nations where people will not be able to afford the increased costs.
- more of the world's food crops will be converted over to fuel production and there will be direct competition between fuel producers and food processors for supplies of wheat, corn, soybean, sugarcane, and other key crops.
- water short countries will divert water from irrigation and increase grain imports to feed their populations. This will reduce their internal (home-grown) supplies of food and make them even more susceptible to the vagaries of the global market.
- more countries with grain deficits.
- more frequent regional famines are a likely further consequence of all of the above.

A Balanced Diet (page 179)

1. Nutrients are required as (a) an energy source and (b) as the raw materials for metabolism, growth, and repair.

2. The new food pyramid distinguishes between "healthy" and "unhealthy" fats, and "healthy" and "unhealthy" (refined) carbohydrate sources. This is contrary to the older pyramid, which placed all fats together as to be avoided, and recommended that all carbohydrates form the base of the food pyramid. The new pyramid recommends a high intake of plant oils which correlate with reduced rates of heart disease.

3. (a) In the Val-de-Marne region, enforced cost constraints were associated with an increase in intakes of fats and sweets and a decrease in fruits and vegetables. There was also some decrease in the consumption of meat, fish, and eggs, but the decrease was not as significant as observed in the fruit and vegetable category.
(b) When money for purchasing food was restricted, most of the calories consumed came from high calorie, nutrient poor foods (sweets and fats). Reduced consumption of fruit, vegetables and protein, will severely deplete the intake of micronutrients. Growth (in children and teenagers), metabolic activities, and the immune system could all be adversely affected. Long term, a micronutrient poor diet has also been linked to diseases such as osteoporosis, cancer and CVD.

4. Obese people are more likely to be malnourished, therefore, their dietary consumption of vitamin D will be less than a person eating a balanced diet. In addition, vitamin D is fat soluble, so will accumulate to greater levels in an obese person reducing bioavailability for metabolism.

Malnutrition and Obesity (page 181)

1. Obesity is regarded as a form of malnutrition because more food is consumed than is required to stay healthy. The food consumed is often highly processed and not nutritionally balanced, containing high levels of fat, sugar, and salt.

2. The two basic energy factors which determine how a persons weight will change are the energy consumed and the energy expended (exercise).

3. (a) Overweight: minimum: 85.6 kg maximum 102.6 kg
(b) Obese: over 102.6 kg

4. (a) Percentage of obese people is lower (up to 50% lower among women) in people with incomes that place them 400% above the poverty line and increases progressively with reduction in income.
(b) Highly educated people will (for the most part) have higher paying jobs than a person with little education. They are able to spend more money on healthy food (fruit, vegetables, lean cuts of meat). They may also know more about the importance of eating a balanced diet to obtain good nutrition, so make better food choices.
(c) A high proportion of people in developing nations live at or below the poverty line and their access to food choices is limited, especially when the foods that are cheapest tend to be those that are nutritionally poor (refined CHO).

5. The root cause of obesity - eating too many calories for energy needs - is often coincident with the consumption of a highly processed (high carbohydrate, high fat) diet. Such diets are poor in vitamins, minerals, and fibre and, even when eaten in excess, provide inadequate nutrition, especially for high needs groups such as young children.

Cardiovascular Disease (page 183)

1. Cardiovascular disease (CVD) refers to a class of diseases that affect the cardiovascular system (the heart or the blood vessels).

2. **Congenital CVD** refers to cardiovascular problems that a person is born with. They can be inherited, the result of viral infections, or the result of genetic defects (mutations). In contrast, **acquired CVD** describes cardiovascular diseases arising during the course of a person's life. They are mostly the result of environmental or lifestyle factors, but can sometimes be the result of genetics.

3. CVD is a major public health concern because it is so widespread, accounting for 34% of deaths in the UK and billions of pounds in lost productivity and heath care costs. Importantly, many of the risk factors associated with CVD are preventable, so education and public health management has a role to play in reducing the levels of CVD in the population.

Atherosclerosis (page 184)

1. Even though a plaque is forming, blood can continue to flow relatively unhindered through blood vessels. It is only when the blood vessel is almost completely obstructed that symptoms arise. Fit, healthy people may not show any symptoms at all until a plaque ruptures and causes a major blood clot, which can be lethal.

2. Atherosclerosis is triggered when a vessel is damaged (e.g. by oxidised LDLs or persistent hypertension). LDLs accumulate at the damaged site and macrophages follow forming foam cells. The foam cells accumulate to form an intermediate lesion called a plaque. As the atheroma develops, the smooth muscle cells of the

blood vessel die, and scar tissue forms. Calcium salts accumulate forming a complicated plaque and the arterial wall may ulcerate. The plaque may break away forming a clot, which may be fatal.

3. People with atherosclerosis are more at risk of suffering an aneurysm, stroke, or heart attack (blood vessels may be blocked from the plaque or a blood clot thrown from a plaque may enter the circulation).

Cholesterol, Diet, and Heart Health (page 185)

1. (a) Cholesterol is essential for the structural and functional integrity of cellular membranes, and it is an important precursor in the synthesis of bile acids, steroid hormones, and fat soluble vitamins, including vitamins A, D, E, and K.
   (b) The body's requirement for cholesterol is met through dietary intake of animal fats and by synthesis within the body (primarily in the liver).

2. (a) LDL deposits cholesterol on the endothelial lining of blood vessels, whereas HDL transports cholesterol to the liver where it is processed. A high LDL:HDL ratio is more likely to result in CVD because more cholesterol will be deposited on blood vessels and contribute to atherosclerosis.
   (b) The LDL:HDL ratio is a more accurate predictor of heart disease risk than total cholesterol *per se*, since it more accurately indicates how much cholesterol will be deposited in arteries.
   (c) The ratio can be lowered in at risk individuals by increasing exercise levels, stopping smoking, losing weight, decreasing consumption of saturated fat, and increasing intake of dietary fibre.

3. (a) In population studies, risk of CVD is decreased when saturated fats and (particularly) *trans*- fats in the diet are reduced (as per the Nurses' Health Study). *Trans*-fats are widespread in highly processed foods because they improve shelf life and make foods more palatable, so reducing intake of processed food is an effective way to reduce *trans*-fat intake.
   (b) Population studies have indicated strong differences in rates of CVD between countries and these differences have been attributed to diet, specifically intakes of saturated fat, salt, and vitamins and antioxidants (the latter two being abundant in fruit and vegetables). Strong north-south gradients in these countries are related to fruit and vegetable consumption, with reduced consumption of fruit and vegetables being associated with higher incidence of CVD (e.g. people in England consume twice as much fruit and a third more vegetables than people in Northern Ireland and have lower rates of CVD).

The Green Revolution (page 187)

1. The first green revolution made use of increased use of machinery, and chemical fertilisers, pesticides, and water, as well as improvements in crop breeds in to increase the yield per unit land from key food crops. This greatly increased global food production but relied heavily on high energy inputs. The second green revolution has employed improved knowledge of plant breeding and genetics to produce high yielding strains with particular desirable qualities (such as disease resistance and drought tolerance) to increase yields further (particularly in tropical countries). Some of this second green revolution (especially more recently) has involved genetic engineering but some has been the result of improved selective breeding practices. This second green revolution is accelerating as a result of genome sequencing in crop varieties, although it is worth noting that continued gains in yield are frequently still reliant on high input agricultural techniques. The further step in the second green revolution is reduce reliance on chemical inputs.

2. (a) **Improve crop yields**:
   Any crop improvements that reduce susceptibility to disease, allow easier crop management, or extend the cultivation range will increase yield. Examples include:
   - Cross breeding parental types to produce semi-dwarf cereal varieties with shorter stems than before. These produce better yields, as dwarf plants use more of their energy for filling the grain than in growing taller. Shorter plants are less likely to fall over, which also increases overall harvest yield (e.g. IR-8 rice)
   - Genetic engineering for disease and pest resistance, e.g. insertion of the Bt gene in corn, cotton, rice, and potatoes provides resistance to insect pests, resistance to powdery mildew in wheat.
   - Genetic engineering for environmental tolerance, e.g. salt tolerance in tobacco.
   - Genetic engineering for herbicide tolerance, e.g. glyphosphate tolerance in maize.

   (b) **Improve crop nutritional value:**
   Genetic engineering to increase micronutrient content of crops, e.g. provitamin A fortification in rice, increased protein content in potatoes, increased lysine content in maize.

3. (a) Recent crop developments could benefit countries suffering food shortages by providing access to high yielding, disease resistant varieties that are tolerant of a wide range of growing conditions. Potentially, new crop varieties could provide more grain, more cheaply, to more people without requiring more land to be under cultivation.
   (b) Developing countries might be unable to take advantage of these improvements if they are farming under sub-optimal conditions (e.g. lacking adequate rainfall or adequate irrigation and without access to manures or the money to purchase inorganic fertilisers.

Selective Breeding in Crop Plants (page 189)

1. (a) Cauliflower: flowers
   (b) Kale: leaf
   (c) Broccoli: inflorescence
   (d) Brussels sprout: lateral buds
   (e) Cabbage: apical (terminal) bud
   (f) Kohlrabi: stem (swollen)

2. If allowed to flower, all six can cross-pollinate.

3. (a) and (b), any two of the following:
   - High yielding crops to maximise crop production.
   - Disease and pest resistant crops lead to increased crop yields and require less pesticide/herbicide application so maximise profit.
   - Fast growing varieties enable the crops to be

harvested more quickly and allow more crops to be planted and harvested in a season.

4. Both methods involve the introduction of a desirable trait (e.g. high yield, drought tolerance) into a plant. Classical selective breeding involves human intervention to physically select and interbreed (cross) two related individuals to produce a new variety or to introduce a desirable trait. Hand pollination and seed harvesting are two examples of this. Modern selective breeding utilises molecular biology techniques to insert desirable traits into a plant. Commonly used techniques include marker assisted selection and genetic modification.

Selective Breeding in Animals (page 191)

1. Inbreeding involves breeding between close relatives, and if practiced over a number of generations lead to increased homozygosity in a population. It is used by animal breeders to 'fix' desirable traits into a population, but an increase in the frequency of recessive, deleterious traits in homozygous form in a population can reduce the health and fitness and of a population and lower fertility levels. Out-crossing involves introducing new (unrelated) genetic material into a breeding line. It is used to increase the genetic diversity, and is used in line-breeding to restore vigour and fertility to a breeding line.

2. Positive outcomes of selective breeding in domestic animals include; desirable traits are established within a relatively short period of time, breeders are able to produce animals with high growth rates, animals can be selected for which produce high yields of meat, wool, or milk, production of animals with good temperament, improve the birthing characteristics of a breed (e.g. easy calving), produce animals specifically suited to the climate or terrain.

   Negative outcomes of selective breeding include; reduction of genetic variability can make the population susceptible to disease or physiological difficulties (e.g. hip displacement), fertility may decrease, the occurrence of deleterious genes becomes more widespread and the breed loses vigour.

3. (a) Genetic gain refers to the gain towards a (reliably attained) desirable phenotype in a breed.
   (b) DNA markers are being used to select breeding stock with desirable carcass characteristics (e.g. high muscle yield in the rump).

4. Increasing the rates of multiple birth in sheep is advantageous in that it increases overall productivity so that the farmer gains more live lambs for every ewe and makes more profit per livestock head. The multiple rates should be of twins however (not triplets); increasing the rates of triplets born is disadvantageous because ewes cannot mother more than two lambs, all lambs will smaller at birth, and survival rates will be compromised, especially if weather conditions are not ideal.

Producing Food with Microorganisms (page 193)

1. **Industrial microbiology** refers to the use of microorganisms, on an industrial scale, for the production of valuable commodities or to carry out some valuable process.

2. Production of alcoholic beverages:
   - Fermentation of fruit sugars by yeasts to produce wine.
   - Grains are first malted and the sugars fermented by yeasts to produce beer.

3. (a) Advantages: it is manufactured from recombinant microorganisms and not extracted from the stomachs of young calves, can be produced in large amounts relatively cheaply, cheese produced using GM chymosin is both vegetarian and kosher so can appeal to a wider market.
   (b) Disadvantages: some consumers perceive food made using GM ingredients as unsafe, chymosin is only one component of calf rennet, so other enzymes may need to be added during cheese making to mimic the 'natural' enzyme profile.

4. The general public often (wrongly) consider all bacteria to be harmful organisms capable of causing disease and illness, and so are wary of their use in food production. Yeast are considered a traditional ingredient as they have been used in the production of fermentation products (e.g. bread) for many thousands of years. Because of this they are more readily accepted by consumers.

Increasing Food Production (page 195)

1. **Advantages**: Increased crop growth rates and yields, production of a disease-free crop, the crop may be more aesthetically pleasing because it has no blemishes and fetch a premium price at the market, pesticides are fast acting and can control large infestations cost effectively,
   Disadvantages: Pesticides kill off all insects including beneficial ones, pesticides can accumulate in the environment and harm the local food chain (including humans), health risks to workers in the industry if pesticides are not handled correctly, pesticide resistance may develop from overuse or incorrect use, fertilisers may enter and contaminate waterways (leading to eutrophication), on a global scale fertiliser application releases greenhouse gases (N_2O).

2. (a) Antibiotics are used in intensive farming systems to prevent, control and treat disease, allowing the production of healthy animals, which in turn allows for faster animal growth.
   (b) The use of antibiotics reduces the amount of disease occurring on intensive farming systems resulting in generally healthier animals overall (given the rearing system). In some cases, the prevention of animal disease may reduce the risk of the disease spreading to humans. Frequent use of antibiotics may result in the development of bacterial resistance, and there is some concern that this resistance may spread to humans. High density farming practices are considered by some to be inhumane and only viable because the use of antibiotics to keep disease at bay.

3. Sustainable agriculture is based on the principle of long term production with minimal environmental impact. It centres around farm management practices that ensure long term productivity and soil health.

4. (a) - (c) any three of the following:
   - Reduced use of fertilisers.
   - Reduced use of pesticides.
   - Smarter irrigation policies to conserve water.
   - Use of integrated pest management schemes.
   - Use of pulse crops and other natural sources for soil nitrification.

5. Sustainable agricultural practices can prove to be more profitable in the long term because they release farmers from the economic treadmill of having to apply increasing amounts of water, fertilisers, and pesticides to the land in order to achieve the same yields. With improved soil health, high energy, expensive inputs can be reduced to a minimum with no reduction in yield, thereby saving money and increasing profits.

Food Preservation (page 197)

1. (a) Heat treatments kill the majority of food spoilage organisms found in food, and by doing so, greatly increase its shelf life (deterioration or rotting of food is the result of microbial activity).
   (b) Heat treatments can sometimes alter the appearance and flavour of food. The degree of alteration is dependent upon the type of food being preserved and the heat treatment which is applied.

2. Sugar and salt both draw water away from the food by the process of osmosis. Without readily available water, the microorganisms on the food cannot grow, the bacterial population dies, and food spoilage is slowed.

KEY TERMS: Word Find (page 198)

O	G	C	A	R	D	I	O	V	A	S	C	U	L	A	R	D	I	S	E	A	S	E	L	V
O	P	V	I	T	A	M	I	N	I	X	C	T	C	H	O	L	E	S	T	E	R	O	L	T
R	B	Z	X	L	M	A	L	N	U	T	R	I	T	I	O	N	D	K	O	H	V	O	X	S
M	J	Y	F	E	R	T	I	L	I	S	E	R	S	S	D	B	S	L	N	G	R	B	K	B
V	A	L	R	I	L	W	D	N	I	E	J	I	O	J	G	E	I	K	X	Q	N	E	H	C
G	B	J	Z	Q	A	P	C	J	Q	B	A	L	A	N	C	E	D	D	I	E	T	S	Z	J
A	T	H	E	R	O	S	C	L	E	R	O	S	I	S	E	H	L	M	B	Z	N	I	H	N
U	X	S	C	O	V	O	W	H	Y	B	R	I	D	V	I	G	O	U	R	Q	F	T	W	Q
Y	Z	R	A	U	V	V	L	K	M	P	Y	Q	G	C	B	J	I	V	C	W	M	Y	D	B
N	S	D	F	L	W	A	J	C	S	T	H	R	R	A	L	P	I	C	K	L	I	N	G	D
I	V	S	F	M	T	R	S	E	L	E	C	T	I	V	E	B	R	E	E	D	I	N	G	X
P	E	S	T	I	C	I	D	E	S	N	P	O	N	Z	M	A	A	S	L	H	D	L	C	Y
R	H	S	J	Q	I	D	N	L	H	A	G	W	T	R	A	N	S	F	A	T	S	D	L	F
C	J	L	O	V	X	B	X	G	Z	L	R	Q	G	E	X	L	F	J	V	Q	Q	A	W	I
N	B	A	D	O	M	E	S	T	I	C	A	T	I	O	N	K	L	U	H	W	D	V	N	F
J	E	H	K	P	F	N	R	K	A	V	R	A	N	T	I	B	I	O	T	I	C	Z	C	P
Z	I	Q	M	C	O	R	O	N	A	R	Y	H	E	A	R	T	D	I	S	E	A	S	E	Q
M	M	G	J	K	X	W	Y	W	F	Q	N	B	O	D	Y	M	A	S	S	I	N	D	E	X

Health vs Disease (page 200)

1. **Disease** describes a condition where all or part of an organism's physiology is disturbed in some way (as a result of infection, an inherited disorder of metabolism, poor diet or lifestyle, or toxins). **Health** is not just the absence of disease, but a state of complete physical, mental, and social well-being.

2. Diseases are usually characterised by a suite of symptoms affecting a number of body systems, and there are many ways in which to view their classification. For example, mental disorders such as anorexia, manifest as deficiency diseases (starvation), and some so-called social diseases, such as STIs are the result of pathogens. Overlap in the causes of disease also leads to confusion over classification, e.g. there is a strong inherited predisposition to alcoholism (a social disease), as well as Alzheimer's and cancers (degenerative diseases).

Infection and Disease (page 201)

1. Robert Koch established a sequence of experimental steps, known as Koch's postulates, for directly relating a specific disease to its specific causative agent.

2. A parasite relies on another organism (the host) for its survival for all or part of its life cycle.

3. Intracellular parasites reside in cells, so it is difficult to control them without also damaging the host cells. In addition, many pass part of their life cycle as cysts, during which they are relatively resistant to treatment.

Transmission of Disease (page 202)

1. A parasite or pathogen benefits from entering a host's body because it offers a regular, easily accessible source of food, and a stable, relatively constant environment in which the parasite or pathogen can complete part or all of its life cycle.

2. (a) and (b) any order: Washing hands after going to the toilet or blowing nose. Sneezing or coughing into a tissue, which is then disposed of, rather than into a hand or into the air.

3. (a) **Malaria**: Transmission by animal (mosquito) vector. Portal of entry is a break in the skin surface. **Note**: This is an example of biological transmission where the vector is part of the pathogen's life cycle.
   (b) **Tetanus**: Transmission by indirect contact (e.g. as when injured with an infected rose thorn). Portal of entry is a break in the skin surface.
   (c) **Cholera**: Waterborne vehicle transmission. Portal of entry is the gastrointestinal tract.
   (d) **Common cold**: Direct contact and droplet transmission. Portal of entry is the respiratory tract.
   (e) **TB**: Droplet transmission. Portal of entry is the respiratory tract.
   (f) **HIV**: Direct contact transmission. Portal of entry are urinogenital openings and breaks in the skin surface.
   (g) **Gonorrhoea**: Direct contact transmission. Portal of entry are urinogenital openings.

Bacterial Pathogens (page 203)

1. (a) - (b) any two of the following:
   - The use of toxins to break down the host cells or connective tissue. This allows the bacteria to spread throughout the body.
   - The bacteria release enzymes to break down clot forming protein fibrin. This allows the bacteria to disperse more readily through the blood system.
   - Fimbriae on the bacterial surface allow it to attach to mucous membranes and attack the host's tissues.

2. (a) **Cholera** is spread by consumption of food or water contaminated with faecal material. The disease can

be controlled by ensuring that all water and food consumed is clean and safe from faecal matter, and that good hygiene practices are followed to further reduce transmission.

(b) **Salmonellosis** is most commonly contracted from eating raw or under-cooked poultry, egg and meat products contaminated with the bacterial genus *Salmonella*. The disease could be controlled by ensuring that all at risk foods were properly stored and cooked, and that safe food hygiene practices were followed to prevent cross contamination with other foods.

3. Airborne diseases are very easily spread when the infected person coughs or sneezes. Immunisation would prevent infection spreading easily by reducing the pool of susceptible people.

Tuberculosis (page 204)

1. (a) When TB bacteria enter the airways, they are ingested by alveolar macrophages and may multiply inside these cells forming tubercles, which may rupture, and result in scarring and cavities filled with necrotic material. Cavities may coalesce and the material inside can be coughed up, passing on the bacteria to others. Scarring and coalescence of cavities with the airways reduces the area for gas exchange and the lung damage and accumulation of dead material leads to a productive cough in which dead material and blood are expelled.
   (b) The material coughed up from the cavities and into the bronchioles contains dead cells but also live bacilli, which are spread easily through airborne transmission to another person.

2. TB is of global concern for a number of reasons. It can be treated with antibiotics, but antibiotic resistance is widespread and increasing, making treatment options difficult for many. Effective treatment requires a long and aggressive course of treatment and non-compliance is common. TB is a widespread and prevalent disease and common in developing countries where capacity to treat it effectively is poorest.

Protozoan Diseases (page 205)

1. (a) A **cyst** is a protective capsule that allows survival of the protozoan when conditions are unfavourable.
   (b) The cyst enables a protozoan to survive because it protects the organism from adverse conditions, allowing the organism to survive outside a host and thus enabling it to reinfect another suitable host.

2. Primary host = *Anopheles* mosquito: Insecta: Diptera (flies), *Anopheles* (some 350 species).

3. (a) Cysts of the *Giardia* parasite are found in water contaminated with faecal material, which often occurs in remote areas without reliable toileting facilities (the parasite also favours conditions where the water is cool, as in forested streams).
   (b) Giardia infection can be avoided by boiling drinking water or sterilising it with iodine.
   (c) Local authorities can prevent *Giardia* becoming a problem by providing adequate toileting facilities near camp sites but well away from water courses and educating people to avoid toileting near streams and rivers.

Malaria (page 206)

1. A mosquito carrying the plasmodium parasite bites a human. The mosquito injects a liquid (saliva) to prevent blood clotting that would block up its mouthparts. The parasite is injected along with the saliva.

2. By removing or destroying the mosquito breeding sites (stagnant water in which mosquito larvae live). This can be achieved by draining ponds and removing car tyres which are notorious for harbouring mosquito larvae. Scientists could assist by introducing mosquito eating fish, e.g. *Gambusia* and rotifers (although the efficacy of these as control agents is now in doubt and mosquito fish themselves are terrible pests).

3. (a) Climate - warm and wet enough for the mosquito vector. Outbreaks are often seasonal and associated with the rainy season when conditions favour transmission. People with no previous exposure (e.g. children) are most at risk.
   (b) The most cost effective measures involve mosquito control, using mosquito nets, and spraying the walls of dwellings with insecticides.

4. The mosquito vectors require high (tropical) regions to breed. A warming climate would provide these conditions over a wider geographical range.

Viral Pathogens (page 207)

1. Host specificity is based on the receptor properties of the viral protein coat. In enveloped viruses, the receptor regions are often glycoprotein spikes which provide a binding site for attachment to the host cell. As the features of the viral capsid or envelope are specific to the receptors of the host cell, only a limited host cell range will be susceptible to infection.

2. (a) Vaccination (immunisation)
   (b) Vaccination will provide artificially acquired active immunity to the disease. However, some viruses (e.g. *Influenzavirus*) acquire mutations (e.g. to their surface proteins) so rapidly that vaccines are difficult to develop and are quickly ineffective against new strains.

The Impact of HIV/AIDS in Africa (page 208)

1. (a) Since the 1980s, life expectancies in most southern African countries have fallen dramatically (from ~56-65 to 40-50 depending on country). For most southern African countries, this sharp decline is due to the impact of HIV/AIDS
   (b) Between 1958 and 1988, life expectancies in most southern African countries increased from around 45 to more than 60 in some cases. This increase was largely the result of health care improvements, namely the availability of antibiotics and the increase in immunisation programmes against common diseases that affected large proportions of the population.

2. Sub-Saharan countries are faced with trying to combat the HIV epidemic while constrained by the loss of much of their productive workforce. AIDS is removing from the population the very people who are required to improve economic well being and public infrastructure. A decline in economic well being leaves sub-Saharan nations at higher risk of food insecurity, increasing debt, and

inability to meet the basic costs of combatting the HIV/ AIDS epidemic. Any recovery programme has to work within these constraints and attempt to provide food and education for its upcoming workforce.

HIV and AIDS (page 209)

1. HIV attacks the very system that normally defends the body from infectious diseases. By knocking out the immune system, it leaves the body vulnerable to invasion by many microbes that would not normally infect a healthy person.
2. (a) The virus rapidly increases in numbers within the first year of infection, followed by a large drop off in numbers in the second year. Over the next 3-10 years, the HIV population gradually increases again.
   (b) The helper T cell numbers respond to the initial infection by increasing in numbers. After about a year, their numbers steadily decrease as they are attacked and destroyed by the HIV.
3. **Transmission of HIV**, any three of: Blood or blood products, vaginal secretions, breast milk, across the placenta, shared needles among intravenous drug users (contaminated with blood from other drug users), sexual intercourse: both homosexual (between males) and heterosexual (between men and women).
4. **HIV positive**: Blood tests have detected the presence of HIV in blood samples from a person (even though they may not have exhibited any symptoms).
5. Blood donated by the public and used to obtain a blood clotting factor (Factor VIII) for haemophiliacs was contaminated with HIV from donors already infected with the virus. This is particularly the case in countries where people are paid to donate blood.
6. HIV mutates very rapidly, changing its protein coat. Any vaccine is quickly rendered useless as the virus has already changed. There are also many different strains of HIV, each requiring a different vaccine.
7. Such people have a genetic makeup and a slightly altered metabolism that does not allow the HIV virus to replicate effectively inside their bodies. By determining how these people are different, it may be possible to develop drugs that mimic the altered metabolism.

Epidemiology of AIDS (page 211)

1. Men are likely to have **multiple partners concurrently**, and **avoid condom use**. **Women have little power** or say in controlling their circumstances and are at risk from partners engaging in risky sexual practices. The lack of employment in rural areas results in an **itinerant population of men**, moving between cities for work and developing sexual networks involving high risk behaviours. They contract HIV and return to spread it through their rural communities.
2. (a) Age structure: A high proportion of individuals of reproductive age are infected (and die) so that the population becomes dominated by non-reproductive individuals (old people and children). Babies, infected *in utero* or during delivery, will also die.
   (b) Local economies will suffer through the removal (or incapacitation) of the sector of the population that normally provides most of the income. This group normally also supports children and elderly, so the economy also bears the cost of caring for the HIV infected, their children, and their old people.
3. Sub-Saharan Africa countries are underdeveloped in their technologies and economies and do not have the resources to fund an expensive and comprehensive AIDS treatment programme. Economically developed countries, which could support such drug programmes, choose not to.
4. **HIV-1**: Recombination of two existing strains of simian immunodeficiency virus (SIV) in a subspecies of common chimpanzee to produce a new strain. There was then cross species transmission of the virus to humans (zoonosis), probably through the handling and consumption of infected chimpanzee carcasses.
   HIV-2: Mutation of an existing simian immunodeficiency virus found in the sooty mangabey (SIV sm). Transmission as above.
5. See column graph below. **Note**: The axis break and change of scale made necessary by the large variability in cases per region and space constraints.

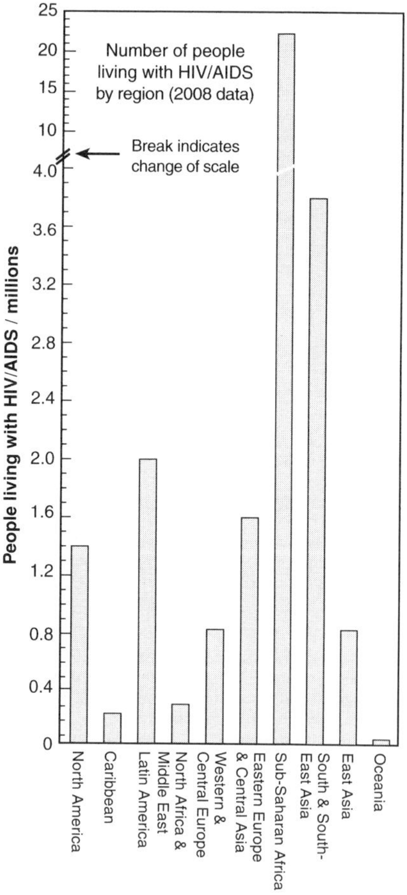

Replication in HIV (page 213)

1. (a) HIV enters a T cell by attaching to the CD4 receptors on the cell surface, and fusing with the cell's plasma membrane.
   (b) Reverse transcriptase transcribes the viral RNA into viral DNA. This must occur for the viral genes to be able to integrate into the host's chromosomes where it stays as a provirus.
   (c) The provirus remains integrated with the host chromosome and persists as a latent infection. This means that it can reinfect new host cells whenever the DNA is replicated.

2. (a) Attachment: The virion adheres to receptor sites on the cell surface. (The attachment structures on the viral surface match the receptors on the host cell).
   (b) Penetration: The host cell engulfs the attached viral particle by endocytosis.
   (c) Uncoating: Host's enzymes degrade the protein coat and release the viral nucleic acid into the cell.
   (d) Biosynthesis: The synthesis (assembly) of new infective virions.
   (e) Release: The active virions are budded off from the host cell by exocytosis.

3. Without reverse transcriptase, the viral RNA cannot be transcribed into viral DNA and it can neither integrate into the host's chromosome nor use the host cell's enzymes to transcribe its genes.

Drug Resistance in HIV (page 214)

1. Factors contributing to the rapid spread of drug resistance in pathogens include:
   - The typically high mutation rates in viruses, bacteria, and protozoa, combined with short generation times (rapid generational turnover).
   - Strong selection pressures imposed by drug use, coupled with misuse of drugs (e.g. using antibiotics against viral infections), poor patient compliance (patients not taking drugs as prescribed), and the poor quality of available drugs (especially to impoverished populations).

2. Resistance may arise though a single mutation or through the accumulation of specific mutations over time. Such mutations may alter the binding capacity of the drug or susceptibility of the virus to the drug. Alternatively, resistance may arise as a result of naturally occurring polymorphisms, which gain favour in the selective environment.

3. Superinfection occurs when an HIV infected person is infected by a second strain of HIV. It appears that the immune system does not recognise the new strain. An HIV vaccine will not be effective if the immune system is incapable of recognising and destroying subsequent HIV invasions.

The Global Threat of Disease (page 215)

1. A zoonosis is a disease arising in humans after crossing the species barrier from another animal (usually as a result of a mutation to the animal pathogen). Such diseases have the potential to cause highly lethal pandemics because they have no previous history in the human population (which will have only limited resistance to them). In addition, because they are new, there is often a considerable lag in identifying the cause and modes of transmission of zoonoses. This can make them more difficult to control quickly.

2. Under suitable conditions, viruses readily exchange genes. The acquisition of new genes from other strains enables new viral subtypes to arise with different compositions of protein on their capsids or envelopes.

3. (a) Swine are susceptible to both avian and swine viruses, both of which can infect humans. The presence of different viral strains within one organism provides the opportunity for viruses to exchange genes and produce a new subtype which could be easily transmitted to humans and potentially lethal.
   (b) Precautions against viral reassortment include not cramping swine into intensive housing situations, restrictions and controls on the importation of swine from other countries or regions, not moving swine when they are obviously unwell or when there is a regional outbreak, quarantining incoming stock.

4. Factory farming situations involve housing stock indoors at high densities, frequently above each other in stacked pens, where the spread of viruses between animals is much easier. Cramped, unsanitary and poorly ventilated conditions also place stock under stress and make them more susceptible to pathogens.

5. A **re-emerging disease**, e.g. TB, is one arising after the pathogen responsible develops resistance to the anti-microbial drugs used to control it. With renewed virulence, the pathogen can then spread rapidly.

6. Drug resistance has allowed the pathogens responsible for largely eradicated diseases, such as TB, to once again become established in the population. When cases appear they are much more difficult to treat and treatment is often ineffective, and this accelerates their spread through the population. In addition, vaccination programmes for some diseases may lapse so that when the disease is encountered again, a large proportion of the population will have no immunity to it.

7. (a) Governments respond to the threat of new flu strains by updating the available vaccine seasonally as new strains arise. In the event of an outbreak of an entirely new strain, authorities respond by **isolation** of those who are already infected, **monitoring** travellers moving between high and low risk regions, and **quarantine** of those who have been exposed to risk. In attempting to contain an outbreak they have the authority to limit public movement and close schools. They also increase the stocks and availability of antiviral drugs.
   (b) Authorities could tighten border security for people and animals who have been exposed to infection. There should be more effective communication between public health and agricultural authorities of disease outbreaks, so that both parties are aware of any potential problems and can take steps to prevent cross-species infections.

8. Discussion of the biological factors acting against the development of an effective HIV vaccine could include:
   – Current vaccine technology works by mimicking natural immunity against reinfection generally seen in individuals recovered from infection; there are no recovered AIDS patients, so there is no natural mechanism to imitate.

- Most vaccines protect against disease, not infection. HIV infection can remain latent for years before causing AIDS.
- Most effective vaccines are whole-killed or live-attenuated pathogens. Killed HIV-1 is not antigenic (produces no antibody response) and a live retroviral vaccine carries a high risk of infection.
- HIV destroys the T cells that are meant to fight it.
- HIV integrates into the host cell's chromosome, where it remains hidden from the immune system.
- HIV exists as many different subtypes, so a vaccine would have to protect against all sub types.
- HIV is highly variable and constantly changing, even within each subtype.

Antigenic Variability in Pathogens (page 217)

1. (a) The viral genome is contained on 8 short, loosely connected RNA segments. This enables ready exchange of genes between different viral strains and leads to alteration on the protein composition of the H and N glycoprotein spikes.
   (b) The body's immune system acquires antibodies to the H and N spikes (antigens) on the viral surface, but when different variants arise they are not recognised nor detected by the immune system (there is no immunological memory for the newly appearing antigens).

2. An antigenic shift represents the combination of two or more different viral strains in a new subtype with new properties and no immunological history in the population. Antigenic drifts are much smaller changes that occur continually over time and to which small adjustments are sufficient to provide resistance.

The Influenza Threat (page 218)

1. The seasonal flu vaccine contains three viral strains, and its composition is determined by the prevalent strains in circulation. Two vaccine formulations are produced each year, one each for the northern and southern hemisphere flu season. The pandemic vaccine is produced only when a new viral strain arises with the potential to cause a pandemic. It is specific to one viral strain only.

2. The influenza viruses are constantly mutating and undergoing gradual genetic change (antigenic drift), so that different viral strains are prevalent each season. These viral mutations prevent the immune system from detecting them. The flu vaccine is updated each year to include the new strains in circulation, so that the immune system will recognise them if an influenza infection occurs, and launch an immune response.

The Control of Disease (page 219)

1. Contagious diseases are those that are easily spread between people (or other animals), whereas non-communicable diseases are not spread between hosts.

2. (a) **Isolation** refers to the containment (in isolation facilities) of people with symptoms of a specific communicable disease so that they do not spread the disease to others. **Quarantine**, in contrast, is the physical isolation of those who are **potentially** infectious (i.e. may be infected) until the time of incubation for infection has passed.
   (b) Isolation and quarantine prevent the spread of a disease by preventing contact of infected or potentially infected people with uninfected individuals. In the case of SARS, immediate quarantine of individuals suspected (but not confirmed) of having the disease helped to contain its spread quickly and effectively.

3. Condoms help to prevent the spread of HIV by presenting a physical barrier to the spread of the virus between people who have sexual contact. HIV requires the transfer of body fluids (including semen).

4. The drainage of stagnant water helps to reduce the breeding areas for the Anopheles mosquito, which is the vector in the transmission of the malarial parasite.

5. (a) **Disinfectants** destroy microbes on non-living surfaces that might otherwise act as sites for transfer of microbes between hosts.
   (b) **Antiseptics** destroy microbes on living surfaces (e.g. skin) thus preventing transfer of microbes between hosts (antiseptics are kinder to skin than disinfectants).
   (c) **Heat** can be used to destroy microbes and/or their toxins, making utensils, food products etc. safe for use or ingestion (inadequate heating of food after storage is a common cause of food poisoning).
   (d) **Ionising radiation** sterilises by directly killing surface microbes. Materials for use (e.g. hospital dressings) must be packaged immediately to protect the sterile environment and prevent recontamination.
   (e) **Desiccation** inhibits the growth of microorganisms by removing water from the growing medium (e.g. food) and so presenting a dry environment in which growth occurs slowly or not at all. NOTE: Most bacteria cannot metabolise and grow when water is absent from the growth medium since water is required to utilise the available energy source. Desiccation can be achieved through the use of high sugar or salt solutions, which effectively reduce available water.
   (f) **Cold** inhibits microbial activity by reducing metabolic rates and therefore slowing growth. The lower the temperature, the slower the growth.

6. (a) Identification of the genetic cause of disease (e.g. the location of the genes associated with particular diseases and disorders) will enable rapid, effective genetic screening for particular diseases using DNA profiling techniques.
   (b) A knowledge of the location of the genes associated with specific disorders and diseases will facilitate the development of gene therapies for the correction of the faulty genes.

7. (a) A proportion of the population choose not to immunise against the disease; the vaccination programme is not 100% effective.
   (b) Vaccination creates a large pool of immune individuals in the population (herd immunity). With so few susceptible individuals, the measles virus is not easily transmitted through the population. **Note**: When the herd immunity effect fails as a result of a fall in vaccination rates, the population as a whole becomes more vulnerable to the disease.

KEY TERMS: Crossword (page 221)

Answers Across
2. Parasite
4. Protozoans
10. Health
12. Incidence
15. Mortality
16. Vector
18. Plasmodium
20. *Mycobacterium tuberculosis*

Answers Down
1. Malaria
3. T Cell
5. Tuberculosis
6. AIDS
7. Koch's postulates
8. *Influenzavirus*
9. Life expectancy
11. Aetiology
13. Retrovirus
14. Prevalence
17. Disease
19. HIV

The First Line of Defence (page 223)

1. The natural population of (normally non-pathogenic) microbes can benefit the host by preventing overgrowth of pathogens (through competitive exclusion).
2. The skin provides a physical barrier to prevent pathogens entering the body. Skin secretions (serum and sweat) contain antimicrobial chemicals that inhibit microbial growth.
3. (a) **Phospholipases** kill bacteria by hydrolysing the phospholipids in cell walls and membranes.
   (b) **Cilia** moves the microbes, which are trapped in mucus towards the mouth and nostrils., where they can be expelled.
   (c) Sebum has antimicrobial activity and (with sweat) a pH that is unfavourable for microbial growth.

The Body's Defences (page 224)

1. **Specific resistance** refers to defence against particular (identified) pathogens. It involves a range of specific responses to the pathogen concerned (antibody production and cell-mediated immunity). In contrast, **non-specific resistance** refers to defence against any type of pathogen. it takes the form of physical and chemical barriers against infection, as well as phagocytosis and inflammation.
2. (a) **Phagocytosis** destroys pathogens directly by engulfing them.
   (b) Antimicrobial substances (e.g. **interferon**) prevent multiplication of microbes (especially viruses).
   (c) Antibodies are produced against specific pathogens, and bind and destroy pathogens or their toxins.
3. A hierarchical system of defence provides a series of back-ups in case a pathogen breaches earlier barriers. Most microbes are excluded by the first line of defence, but those that penetrate the skin will usually be destroyed by white blood cells and the chemicals associated with inflammation. Failing this, the body will mount a targeted specific defence against the identified pathogen still remaining.

The Action of Phagocytes (page 225)

1. Neutrophils, eosinophils, macrophages.
2. By looking at the ratio of white blood cells to red blood cells (not involved in the immune response). An elevated white blood cell count (specifically a high neutrophil count) indicates microbial infection.
3. Microbes may be able to produce toxins that kill phagocytes directly. Others can enter the phagocytes, completely filling them and preventing them functioning or remaining dormant and resuming activity later.

Inflammation (page 226)

1. (a) **Increased diameter and permeability of blood vessels**. Purpose: Increases blood flow and delivery of leucocytes to the area. Aids removal of destroyed microbes or their toxins. Allows defensive substances to leak into the tissue spaces.
   (b) **Phagocyte migration and phagocytosis**. Purpose: To directly attack and destroy invading microbes and foreign substances.
   (c) **Tissue repair**. Purpose: Replaces damaged cells and tissues, restoring the integrity of the area.
2. Phagocytic features: Ability to squeeze through capillary walls (amoeboid movement), and ability to engulf material by phagocytosis.
3. Histamines and prostaglandins attract phagocytes to the site of infection.
4. **Pus** is the accumulated debris of infection (dead phagocytes, damaged tissue, and fluid). It accumulates at the site of infection where the defence process is most active.

Fever (page 227)

1. The high body temperature associated with fever intensifies the action of interferon (a potent antiviral substance). Fever also increases metabolism, which is associated with increased blood flow. These changes increase the rate at which white blood cells are delivered to the site of infection and help to speed up the repair of tissues. The release of interleukin-1 during fever helps to increase the production of T cell lymphocytes and speeds up the immune response.
2. **1**: Macrophage ingests a microbe and destroys it.
   2: The release of endotoxins from the microbe induces the macrophage to produce interleukin-1 which is released into the blood.
   3: Interleukin-1 travels in the blood to the hypothalamus of the brain where it stimulates the production of large amounts of prostaglandins.
   4: Prostaglandins cause resetting of the thermostat to a higher temperature, causing fever.

The Lymphatic System (page 228)

1. **Lymph** has a similar composition to tissue fluid but has more leucocytes (derived from lymphoid tissues). **Note**: Tissue fluid is similar in composition to plasma (i.e. containing water, ions, urea, proteins, glucose etc.) but lacks the large proteins found in plasma.
2. Lymph returns tissue fluid to general circulation, and with the blood, circulates lymphocytes around the body.
3. (a) **Lymph nodes**: Filter foreign material from the lymph by trapping it in fibres.
   They also produce lymphocytes.
   (b) **Bone marrow**: Produces many kinds of white blood cells: monocytes, macrophages, neutrophils, eosinophils, basophils, T and B lymphocytes.

The Immune System (page 229)

1. (a) **Humoral immune system**: Production of antibodies against specific antigens. The antibodies disable circulating antigens.
   (b) **Cell-mediated immune system**: Involves the production of T cells which destroy pathogens or their toxins by direct contact or by producing substances that regulate the activity of other cells in the immune system.
2. In the bone marrow (adults) or liver (foetuses).
3. (a) Bone marrow (b) Thymus
4. (a) **Memory cells**: Retain an antigen memory. They can rapidly differentiate into antibody- producing plasma cells if they encounter the same antigen again.
   (b) **Plasma cells**: Secrete antibodies against antigens (very rapid rate of antibody production).
   (c) **Helper T cells**: Activate cytotoxic T cells and other helper T cells. Also needed for B cell activation.
   (d) **Suppressor T cells**: Regulate the immune system response by turning it off when antigens disappear.
   (e) **Delayed hypersensitivity T cells**: Cause inflammation in allergic responses and are responsible for rejection of transplanted tissue.
   (f) **Cytotoxic T cells**: Destroy target cells on contact (by binding and lysing cells).
5. **Immunological memory**: The result of the differentiation of B cells after the first exposure to an antigen. Those B cells that differentiate into long lived memory cells are present to react quickly and vigorously in the event of a second infection.

Antibodies (page 231)

1. **Antibodies** are proteins produced in response to antigens; they recognise and bind antigens. **Antigens** are foreign substances (often proteins) that promote the formation of antibodies (invoke an immune response).
2. (a) The immune system must be able to recognise self from non-self so that it can recognise foreign material (and destroy it) and its own tissue (and not destroy it).
   (b) During development, any B cells that react to the body's own antigens are selectively destroyed. This process leads to self tolerance.
   (c) Autoimmune disease (disorder).
   (d) Any two of: Grave's disease (thyroid enlargement), rheumatoid arthritis (primarily joint inflammation), insulin-dependent diabetes mellitus (caused by immune destruction of the insulin-secreting cells in the pancreas), haemolytic anaemia (premature destruction of red blood cells), and probably multiple sclerosis (destruction of myelin around nerves).
3. Antibodies inactivate pathogens in four main ways: **Neutralisation** describes the way in which antibodies bind to viral binding sites and bacterial toxins and stop their activity. Antibodies may also **inactivate particulate antigens**, such as bacteria, by sticking them together in clumps. Soluble antigens may be bound by antibodies and fall out of solution (**precipitation**) so that they lose activity. Antibodies also activate **complement** (a defence system involving serum proteins), tagging foreign cells so that they can be recognised and destroyed.
4. (a) **Phagocytosis**: Antibodies promote the formation of inactive clumps of foreign material that can easily be engulfed and destroyed by a phagocytic cell.
   (b) **Inflammation**: Antibodies are involved in activation of complement (the defence system involving serum proteins which participate in the inflammatory response and other immune system activities).
   (c) **Bacterial cell lysis**: Antibodies are involved in tagging foreign cells for destruction and in the activation of complement (the defence system involving serum proteins which participate in the lysis of foreign cells).

Acquired Immunity (page 233)

1. (a) **Passive immunity** describes the immunity that develops after antibodies are transferred from one person to another. In this case, the recipient does not make the antibodies themselves.
   (b) **Naturally acquired** passive immunity arises as a result of antibodies passing from the mother to the foetus/infant via the placenta/breast milk. **Artificially acquired** passive immunity arises as a result of injection with immune serums e.g. in antivenoms.
2. (a) Newborns need to be supplied with maternal antibodies because they have not yet had exposure to the everyday microbes in their environment and must be born with operational defence mechanisms.
   (b) The antibody "supply" is (ideally) supplemented with antibodies in breast milk because it takes time for the infant's immune system to become fully functional. During this time, the supply of antibodies received during pregnancy will decline.
   (c) Breast feeding provides your infant with a naturally acquired passive immunity to help protect it against infections while its immune system develops. Without this acquisition, your infant is more likely to be vulnerable to everyday infections against which you already have immunity but he/she does not.
3. (a) **Active immunity** is immunity that develops after the body has been exposed to a microbe or its toxins and an immune response has been invoked.
   (b) **Naturally acquired** active immunity arises as a result of exposure to an antigen such as a pathogen, e.g. natural immunity to chickenpox. **Artificially acquired** active immunity arises as a result of vaccination, e.g. any childhood disease for which vaccinations are given: diphtheria, measles, mumps, polio etc.
4. (a) The primary response is less pronounced (smaller magnitude) than the secondary response. The primary response takes longer to develop and is over more quickly than the secondary response, which is rapid and long lasting.
   (b) The immune system has already been prepared to respond to the antigen by the first exposure to it. When the cells of the immune system receive a second exposure to the same antigen they can respond quickly with rapid production of antibodies.
5. (a) Herd immunity refers to the protection that unimmunised people have against a circulating disease by virtue of the fact that most of the population are immunised.
   (b) A fall in vaccination rates is a concern because, once the population contains a high proportion of

non-vaccinated people, herd immunity is lost and a circulating disease can spread very rapidly through the community, raising public health costs and contributing to lost productivity.

Vaccines and Vaccination (page 235)

1. **Attenuated viruses** are more effective in the long term because they tend to replicate in the body, and the original dose therefore increases over time. Such vaccines are derived from mutations accumulated over time in a laboratory culture, so there is always a risk that they will back-mutate to a virulent form.

2. (a) High vaccination rates increase the rates of immunity within a population, so fewer people will contract the disease with each outbreak. Transmission of the disease is limited because there are fewer susceptible hosts for the disease to exploit, until eventually the disease no longer occurs in the population.
   (b) The success of the smallpox eradication programme was largely due to carefully monitored vaccination programmes together with strict surveillance of outbreaks which were then contained by isolating patients and even villages. Authorities responded quickly to investigate and limit outbreaks. In addition, humans were the only reservoir and there were no carriers, so it was easier to know when the disease was eradicated from a region.
   (c) Tuberculosis frequently remains dormant in infected people often for long periods of time, and only surfaces as active TB when their immune system is weakened. This means that it is difficult to locate all carriers of the disease and containment is not easily achievable without huge resources.

3. Several research institutions maintain the smallpox virus for ongoing research. Smallpox researchers must be vaccinated to prevent accidental contamination. More recently there have been concerns about the smallpox virus being used as a weapon in bioterrorism.

4. The number of reported cases of whooping cough increased significantly. They only began to drop again when vaccination rates increased again.

New Medicines (page 237)

1. Some 120 drugs commonly used today are derived from plants, many of them from just a few species of tropical plants. Given that there are some 300 000 plus species of plants on Earth, the potential to discover and harvest new medicines from plants is vast, and thus far largely unrealised.

2. The majority of plant based medicines to date have been extracted from tropical plants. The loss of tropical plant biodiversity may mean that plant species are lost before we have had an opportunity to screen them for potential new medicines, and limit the number of new medicine discoveries.

3. Extracted compounds are placed onto a bacterial agar plate and incubated. A clear zone around the compound indicates antimicrobial activity. The size of the clear zone can be used as an indication of the compound's effectiveness in inhibiting growth of specific microbes.

4. Bacterial resistance to traditional antibiotics is increasing. Alternative antibiotics (e.g. from plants) will provide a new range of effective drugs which the microbes have not yet encountered, therefore they will have no resistance to them.

Living with Chronic Lung Disease (page 242)

1. The economic impact of tobacco smoking-related diseases is two fold. Directly there are the considerable health costs associated with treating the consequences of diseases such as chronic bronchitis and emphysema, which often require repeated and prolonged hospital visits. Secondly, there is the economic cost of lost work days (estimated 24 million lost work days per annum).

2. This response is largely a student's own and there is no 'right' answer. Tobacco-related diseases generally have a detrimental effect on a person's quality of life and on the quality of life for those who end up as carers for debilitated relatives. There are additional associated health costs with hospital and doctor's visits and treatments, and the stress of living with a chronic condition which leaves the sufferer vulnerable to more serious lung infections. Personal testimonials, such as that from Jenny's daughter, provide a first hand account of what the personal costs can be and may give some people enough reason to reconsider their smoking habit or to stop them ever taking it up.

Respiratory Diseases (page 243)

1. Obstructive lung diseases are those in which the air cannot reach the gas exchange region of the lung, as occurs as a result of airway constriction (asthma), excess mucus (bronchitis), or reduced lung elasticity (emphysema). Restrictive lung diseases result from scarring of the gas exchange surface (fibrosis) which results in stiffening and lack of lung expansion. Such diseases result from inhalation of dusts (e.g. coal dust).

2. (a) In a chronic obstructive pulmonary disease, the FEV1 is reduced disproportionately more than the FVC resulting in an FEV1/FVC ratio less than 70%.
   (b) Although the FEV1/FVC ratio is reduced in asthmatics, there will be an improvement in the ratio towards the normal range (80%+) after treatment.
   (c) In a restrictive lung disease, both FEV1 and the FVC are compromised equally, so even though measures of lung function indicate impairment the FEV1/FVC ratio remains high.

3. Restrictive lung diseases, such as fibrosis, impair lung function because the gas exchange surface becomes scarred, less flexible, and thicker. This reduces the amount of alveolar expansion possible and reduces the diffusion efficiency across the gas exchange surface.

4. Many restrictive diseases are caused by inhalation of dusts and pollutants associated with particular occupations, e.g. asbestos workers, coal miners, beryllium miners, cement workers etc.

5. Tobacco smoking destroys supporting tissues in the small airways and leads to the production of excess mucus (as the body tries to rid the lungs of the irritants). These effects lead to the symptoms of emphysema and chronic bronchitis respectively so the diseases usually occur together in smokers.

Smoking and the Lungs (page 245)

1. Long-term smoking results in increased production of mucus (in an attempt to trap and rid the lungs of smoke particles). This lung tissue is irritated and a cough develops associated with removing the excess mucus. The smoke particles indirectly destroy the alveolar walls, leading to coalescing of the alveoli and a substantial loss of lung surface area. The toxins in the smoke and tar damage the DNA of cells and lead to cancerous cells and tumours.

2. (a) **Tars**: Cause chronic irritation of the respiratory system and are also carcinogenic
   (b) **Nicotine**: Addictive component of tobacco smoke
   (c) **Carbon monoxide**: Markedly reduces the oxygen carrying capacity of the blood by binding to haemoglobin and forming a stable carboxy-haemoglobin compound. CO has a very high affinity for Hb (higher than that of oxygen) and will preferentially occupy oxygen binding sites. It is released only slowly for the body.

3. (a) **Emphysema**: Increasing shortness of breath (which becomes increasingly more severe until it is present even at rest). Chest becomes barrel shaped (associated with air being trapped in the outer part of the lungs). Often accompanied by a chronic cough and wheeze (caused by the distension (damage and coalescing) of the alveoli). **Note**: Chronic bronchitis and emphysema are often together called chronic obstructive lung disease.
   (b) **Chronic bronchitis**: A condition in which sputum (phlegm) is coughed up on most days during at least three consecutive months in at least two consecutive years. The disease results in widespread narrowing and obstruction of the airways in the lungs and often occurs with or contributes to emphysema.
   (c) **Lung cancer**: Impaired lung function; coughing up blood, chest pain, breathlessness, and death.

4. (a) A long term study is important with a chronic disease that develops slowly because it may take many years for convincing relationships to become evident in the data.
   (b) The study also showed that there was a convincing 20 year lag in the development of lung cancer in smokers.

Smoking and the Cardiovascular System (page 247)

1. (a) Smoking damages arteries and contributes to hypertension, peripheral vascular disease, and the formation of atherosclerotic plaques. Narrowing of the arteries causes the heart to work harder to supply oxygen to the tissue, yet this is compromised by the carbon monoxide load in the blood.
   (b) Tobacco smoking greatly increases the risk of CVD because it works synergistically with other risk factors. Any given risk factor (e.g. high LDL:HDL ratio) has a proportionately greater effect in a smoker than in a non-smoker.
   (c) The evidence linking cigarette smoking to increased incidence of CVD is clear and convincing. The incidence of CVD in smokers is much higher than in non-smokers, especially when there are other risk factors present. For example, in data relating to percentage of deaths in people with hypertension and high cholesterol, declines in mortality were closely associated with declines in percentage of those smoking. Note that the deaths attributable to smoking in the obese do not decline with declines in smoking rates, indicating a more complicated combination of risk factors in which obesity is clearly contributing significantly to the overall risk.

2. Nicotine causes arterial constriction, raising blood pressure and heart rate. It also mobilises fat stores. Carbon monoxide displaces oxygen from haemoglobin, so it markedly reduces the carrying capacity of the blood. In addition, both nicotine and carbon monoxide increase the viscosity of the blood, making clots more likely. All these effects contribute to the heart having to work harder to deliver adequate oxygen to the tissues through constricted vessels.

3. (a) Controllable risk factors often occur together because some tend to be causative for others, or at least always associated, e.g. obesity greatly increases the risk of high blood lipids and high blood pressure: all factors increase the risk of CVD.
   (b) Those with several risk factors have a higher chance of developing CVD because the risks are cumulative and add up to pose a greater total risk.

Global Biodiversity (page 250)

1. Species diversity refers to the number of different species within an area (species richness), while genetic diversity describes the diversity of genes within a particular species. Biodiversity is defined as the measure of all genes, species, and ecosystems in a region, so both genetic and species diversity are important in determining a region's total biodiversity.

2. Consideration of ecosystem diversity is very important when considering areas to set aside for conservation purposes because regions with diverse ecosystems will have higher levels of species richness, and the two measures are interdependent. A loss of habitat diversity will have a negative impact on the species richness of an area, and habitat diversity itself is contingent on species richness. Loss or decline in one will invariably result in loss or decline in the other.

3. The hotspot list is as follows:

1 **Tropical Andes**
The richest and most diverse hotspot where it is home to 20 000 endemic plants and at least 1500 endemic non-fish vertebrates.

2 **Sundaland**
Some of the largest islands in the world are found here in Southeast Asia. The second-richest hotspot in endemic plants, and well known for its mammalian fauna, which includes the orangutan.

3 **Mediterranean basin**
The site of many ancient and modern civilisations, it is the archetype and largest of the five Mediterranean-climate hotspots (also see nos. 9, 12, 19 and 22). One of the hotspots most heavily affected by human activity, it has 13 000 endemic plants, and is home to a number of interesting vertebrates such as the Spanish ibex.

4 **Madagascar and Indian Ocean islands**
Madagascar is a top conservation priority as this 'mini-continent' has undergone extensive deforestation. This hotspot is famous for reptiles such as chameleons and is home to all the world's lemur species.

5 **Indo-Burma**
An area stretching from the eastern slopes of the Himalayas through Burma and Thailand to Indochina. This region hosts the world's highest freshwater turtle diversity (43 species), and a diverse array of mammals. Several new ungulate species, such as the saola and giant muntjac, were recently discovered here.

6 **Caribbean**
One of the highest concentrations of species per unit area on Earth. Reptiles are particularly diverse (497 species are found here), 80 percent of which are found nowhere else. Non-fish vertebrates number 1518.

7 **Atlantic Forest region**
Once covering an area nearly three times the size of California, the Atlantic Forest has been reduced to about 7% of its original extent. It is most famous for 25 different kinds of primates, 20 of which are endemic. Among its best-known 'flagship species' are the critically endangered muriquis and lion tamarins.

8 **Philippines**
The most devastated of the hotspots, the forest cover has been reduced to 3% of its original extent. The Philippines is especially rich in endemic mammals and birds, such as the Philippine eagle.

9 **Cape Floristic Province**
This Mediterranean-type hotspot in southern Africa covers an area roughly the size of Ireland, and is now approximately 20% of its original extent. It is home to 8200 plant species, more than 5500 of which are endemic.

10 **Mesoamerica**
Forming a land bridge between two American continents, this hotspot features species representative of North and South America as well as its own unique biota. The spider and howler monkeys, Baird's tapir and unusual horned guan are 'flagship species'.

11 **Brazilian Cerrado**
A vast area of savanna and dry forest, the Cerrado is Brazil's new agricultural frontier and has been greatly altered by human activity in the past few decades. Home to 4400 endemic plants and several well-known mammal species, including the giant anteater, Brazilian tapir, and maned wolf.

12 **Southwest Australia**
A Mediterranean-type system, this hotspot is rich in endemic plants, reptiles, and marsupials including numbat, honey possum and quokka. It is also home to some of the world's tallest trees, e.g. giant eucalyptus.

13 **Mountains of South-Central China**
An area of extreme topography, these mountains are home to several of the world's best-known mammals, including the giant panda, the red panda, and the golden monkey. This hotspot is largely unexplored and may hold many undiscovered species.

14 **Polynesia/Micronesia**
This hotspot comprises thousands of tiny islands scattered over the vast Pacific, from Fiji and Hawaii to Easter Island and is noteworthy for its land snails, birds, and reptiles. Hawaii has suffered some of the most severe extinctions in modern history, due in part to the introduction of non-native plant and animal species.

15 **New Caledonia**
One of the smallest hotspots yet it has the largest concentration of unique plants with five plant families found nowhere else on Earth. This hotspot also features many endemic birds, such as the kagu, a long-legged, flightless forest dweller representing an entire family.

16 **Choco-Darien Western Ecuador**
Some of the world's wettest rain forests are found here, and amphibians, plants and birds are particularly abundant. It has one of the highest levels of endemism of any hotspot with 210 endemic amphibian species of the 350 species found here.

17 **Guinean Forests of West Africa**
(in error, this hotspot was not numbered on the map). With the highest mammalian diversity of any hotspot, these forests are home to the rare pygmy hippopotamus and many other striking species, including the western chimpanzee, Diana monkey and several forest duikers. The numbers of these endemic mammals have been severely reduced by large-scale logging and hunting.

18 **Western Ghats/Sri Lanka**
The Western Ghats mountain chain and adjacent island of Sri Lanka harbour high concentrations of endemic reptiles; of 259 reptile species, 161 are found nowhere else on Earth. This hotspot is also home to a number of 'flagship species', including the lion-tailed macaque.

19 **California Floristic Province**
Extending along the coast of California and into Oregon and northwestern Baja California, Mexico, this is one of five hotspots featuring a Mediterranean-type climate of hot, dry summers and cool, wet winters. It is especially rich in plants, with more than 4000 plant species, almost half of which are endemic.

20 **Succulent Karoo**
The only arid hotspot, the Succulent Karoo of southern Africa is renowned for unique succulent plants, as well as lizards and tortoises. in Namaqualand, in the southern part of this hotspot, a seasonal burst of bloom in September attracts many tourists.

21 **New Zealand**
This hotspot claims a number of world-famous endemic bird species, including kiwi (a nocturnal, flightless bird), takahe (a diurnal, flightless bird), and the critically endangered kakapo (a large, flightless parrot).

22 **Central Chile**
This hotspot features an arid region as well as a more typical Mediterranean-type zone. Best known for its incredible variety of plant species but also features unusual fauna, including one of the largest birds in the Americas, the Andean condor.

23 **Caucasus**
Situated between the Black Sea and the Caspian Sea, Caucasus habitats range from temperate forests to grasslands. A diversity of plants have been recorded here with some 6300 species, more than 1600 of which are endemic.

24 **Wallacea**
Named for the 19th century naturalist Alfred Russel

Wallace, this hotspot comprises the large Indonesian island of Sulawesi, the Moluccas and many smaller islands. The area is particularly rich in endemic mammals and birds.

25 **Eastern Arc Mountains/ Coastal Forests of Tanzania and Kenya**
A chain of upland and coastal forests, this hotspot claims one of the densest concentrations of endemic plant and primate species in the world. It is home to African violets and 4000 other plant species, as well as the 1500 remaining Kirk's red colobus monkeys.

Britain's Biodiversity (page 251)

1. Table and graph below:

	% of species		Key
Protozoa	22.8%	(82°)	
Algae	22.8%	(82°)	
Fungi	17.1%	(62°)	
Ferns & bryophytes	1.2%	(4°)	
Lichens	1.7%	(6°)	
Flowering plants	1.6%	(6°)	
Invertebrates	32.5%	(117°)	
Vertebrates	0.3%	(1°)	

Proportion of British species in different taxonomic groups

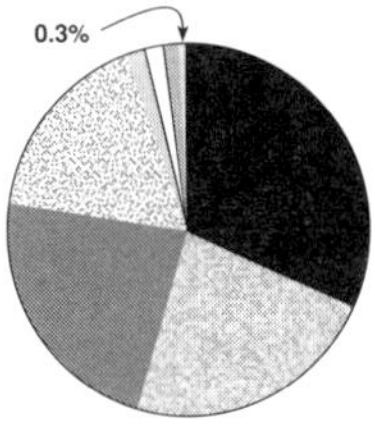

2. Invertebrate phyla, protozoans, algae, and lower plants show a much higher biodiversity than the higher plants and vertebrate taxa.

3. (a) Our knowledge of the biodiversity of invertebrate animals and bacteria (especially the latter) is poor compared with that of vertebrates i.e. there are many more undescribed species, and there is doubt as to how many species actually exist.
   (b) Vertebrates are large, conspicuous organisms with (for the most part) sexual reproduction. This makes determination of "a species" relatively simple even if morphology is similar.

4. The UK has a low level of endemism. It is not far from the European continent ; this facilitates species transfers. In addition, its isolation from the continental land mass has been limited for much of its geologic history (isolation is required for endemism to develop).

5. (a) 12 000 – 3800 = 8200
   8200 ÷ 12 000 X 100 = 68.3%. Nearly 70% decline.
   (b) The barn owl is widely distributed, so the population does not have the problems associated with scattered or isolated distribution. The causes of decline have been identifiable and manageable in that rather simple measures can be taken to increase survival rates of both the young and breeding adults. They are also relatively adaptable birds, taking a variety of prey and responding well to habitat enhancement (e.g. using new nest sites).

Measuring Diversity in Ecosystems (page 253)

1. (a) **Species richness** measures the number of species within an ecosystem, whereas **species evenness** describes how equably the species are distributed within an ecosystem.
   (b) Both measures are important when considering species conservation. Species richness could give an indication of ecosystem stability, and therefore how at-risk particular species may be. Species evenness provides an indication of the species distribution (a limited distribution or a distribution where individuals are widely separated may indicate the species is at risk).

2. Sampling must be unbiased in order to provide a reliable representation of the ecosystem. This is usually achieved by random sampling. The sample size must be large enough to reliably record the species present, and the sampling method used must enable us to collect the information required by the study.

3. High diversity systems have a greater number of biotic interactions operating to buffer them against change (the loss or decline of one component (species) is less likely to affect the entire ecosystem). With a large number of species involved, ecosystem processes, such as nutrient recycling, are more efficient and less inclined to disruption.

4. Species diversity index used in (any of):
   - Comparisons of similar ecosystems which have been subjected to (beneficial or detrimental) human influence (e.g. restoration or pollution).
   - Assessment of the same ecosystem before and after some event (fire, flood, pollution, environmental restoration).
   - Assessment of the same ecosystem along some environmental gradient (e.g. distance from a point source of pollution).
   - Assessment of the biodiversity value of an area for the purposes of management or preservation (tends to be a political lobbying point).

5. (a) Species richness
   Site 1: 6 Site 2: 6 Site 3: 5
   (b) Species evenness
   Site 1: >1 Site 2: =1 Site 3: >>1
   (c) Simpson's index
   Site 1: 0.722 Site 2: 0.812 Site 3: 0.479
   Whole stream: 0.888

Loss of Biodiversity (page 255)

1. Loss of biodiversity from an ecosystem has a cascade effect to the remaining species. The effects depend very much on the species that disappears (e.g. predator, producer) but, in general, species loss results in altered food chains and food webs, allowing for the proliferation of some species and the demise of others. Other changes include a loss of stability and resilience,

and disruption to normal processes, interactions and outcomes, such as nutrient cycling, soil formation, pollination, oxygen production, carbon sequestration and climate regulation.

Characteristics of Life (page 256)

1. Three of: cytoplasm (nutrient "soup"), plasma membrane, genetic material, metabolism.

2. (a) **Size**: Viruses are very small: generally 50-500 times smaller than a typical prokaryotic cell and up to 5000 times smaller than a eukaryote cell.
   (b) **Metabolism**: Cells have metabolic activity; there are chemical reactions taking place much of the time. A virus has no cytoplasm and no metabolism of its own. It relies on the metabolism of its host cell.
   (c) **Organelles**: Viruses have no organelles unlike cells, most of which have organelles which carry out specific roles in the cell.
   (d) **Genetic material**: Viruses have a single or double stranded chromosome which can be RNA or DNA. Cells have only double stranded DNA chromosomes. In eukaryotes the chromosomes are contained within a nuclear membrane.
   (e) **Life cycle**: Outside a living cell, viruses exist as inert particles, adopting a "living" programme only when they invade a host cell and take over the cellular machinery. At times, they may integrate into the host cell's chromosome and remain latent. Cells are generally either "alive" (when there is metabolic activity) or dead (no metabolic activity). **Note**: There are exceptions to this generalisation, e.g. bacterial endospores, which are special resting stages with no metabolic activity.

3. Multicellular organisms are said to show emergent properties because they have properties that go beyond those of a single cell or unicellular organism, e.g. specialised cell types with differing functions.

Types of Living Things (page 257)

1. (a) **Autotrophic**: Plant cells, some protoctistan cells, some bacterial cells.
   (b) **Heterotrophic**: Fungal cells, animal cells, some protoctistan cells, some bacterial cells, viruses.

2. (a) Prokaryotic cells are much smaller (and simpler) than the cells of eukaryotes.
   (b) Prokaryotic cells are bacterial cells while eukaryotic cells are all cell types other than bacteria and viruses. Prokaryotes lack a distinct nucleus, have no membrane-bound organelles, have a cell wall usually containing peptidoglycan and their DNA is present as a single, naked chromosome.

3. (a) Fungi are plant-like in their appearance and habit (growth form, lack of movement, habitat etc.).
   (b) This classification was erroneous because fungi (unlike plants) lack chlorophyll, their cell walls contain chitin (not cellulose), and they are heterotrophic (not autotrophic).

4. Protoctistans often exhibit both animal-like and plant-like features and the group is very diverse in terms of nutrition, reproduction, and structure. **Note**: From a phylogenetic point of view, the protoctists are not monophyletic and should be classified accordingly.

Types of Cells (page 258)

1. (a) **Plant cells**: Mesophyll cell, vessel element (note that this is a dead cell), guard cells.
   (b) **Characteristics**: Cellulose cell wall, chloroplasts containing chlorophyll*s*, carbohydrate stored as starch, large vacuoles.

2. (a) **Animal cells**: Osteocyte, leucocyte, smooth muscle cell, epidermal cells of skin, neurone, erythrocyte.
   (b) **Characteristics**: No cellulose cell wall, no chloroplasts or plastids of any kind, vacuoles if present are small, no regular geometric shape.

3. (a) **Protoctistans**: *Amoeba, Euglena, Paramecium, Spirogyra.*
   (b) **Characteristics**: A very diverse group (the eukaryotes that do not fit into plant, animal, or fungi classification). Generally refers to unicellular eukaryotes, although some primitive multicellular organisms have been included in recent years. Includes protozoans which are heterotrophic (animal-like in their nutrition), and algae, which have chloroplasts and are autotrophic (plant-like in their nutrition). A difficult group to give general characteristics for because they are so diverse. Often ciliated (e.g. *Paramecium*) or flagellated (e.g. *Euglena*). Note that the cyanobacteria are now classified within Prokaryotae (not Protoctista).

4. (a) **Fungal cells**: Yeast, pin mould hyphae.
   (b) **Characteristics**: Eukaryotes, usually multicellular, all are heterotrophs (no photosynthetic ability), lack chloroplasts. Except in yeasts, the basic fungus body is composed of basic building blocks called hyphae. Cell walls composed mainly of chitin.

5. (a) **Prokaryotae**: *Cyanobacteria*, *Diplococcus* bacteria, *Bacillus* bacteria.
   (b) **Characteristics**: Prokaryotes (single, circular chromosome not contained within a nuclear membrane), cell wall containing peptidoglycan, extra-chromosomal material present (plasmids), some capable of forming resistant endospores.

Unicellular Eukaryotes (page 264)

1. Summary for each organism under the given headings:

   Amoeba:
   Nutrition: Heterotrophic, food (e.g. bacteria) ingested by phagocytosis. Food digested in food vacuoles.
   Movement: By pseudopodia (cytoplasmic projections).
   Osmoregulation: Contractile vacuole.
   Eye spot: Absent.
   Cell wall: Absent.

   Paramecium:
   Nutrition: Heterotrophic (feeds on bacteria and small protoctists). Food digested in food vacuoles.
   Movement: By beating of cilia.
   Osmoregulation: Contractile vacuoles.
   Eye spot: Absent.
   Cell wall: Absent.

   Euglena:
   Nutrition: Autotrophic (photosynthetic), but can be heterotrophic when light deprived.
   Movement: By flagella (one larger, which is labelled, and one very small, beside the gullet).
   Osmoregulation: Contractile vacuole.

Eye spot: Present.
Cell wall: Absent, although there is a wall-like pellicle, which lies inside the plasma membrane and is flexible.

Chlamydomonas:
Nutrition: Autotrophic (photosynthetic).
Movement: By flagella.
Osmoregulation: Contractile vacuole.
Eye spot: Present.
Cell wall: Present.

2. *Amoeba*, *Paramecium*, *Euglena*, *Chlamydomonas.*

3. An eye spot enables an autotroph to detect light and so move into well lit regions where it can photosynthesise.

Classification System (page 265)

1. (a) 1. Kingdom 2. Phylum 3. Class 4. Order 5. Family 6. Genus 7. Species
   (b) 1. Animal 2. Chordata 3. Mammalia 4. Primates 5. Hominidae 6. *Homo* 7. *sapiens*

2. A two part naming system where the first word (capitalised and italicised) denotes the genus and the second word (lower case and italicised) denotes the species. Sometimes a third word (also lower case and italicised) denotes a subspecies.

3. (a) and (b) in any order:
Avoid confusion over the use of common names for organisms; provide a unique name for each type of organism; attempt to determine/define the evolutionary relationship of organisms (phylogeny).

4. Any of the following:
DNA profiling/sequencing: Where the unique genetic makeup of an individual is revealed and used for comparisons with related organisms.
DNA hybridisation: Where the percentage DNA similarity between organisms is compared.
Amino acid sequencing: Where the number of amino acid differences between organisms are compared.
Immunological distance: Indirectly estimate the degree of similarity of proteins in different species.

5. (a) **Monotreme**: Egg laying with little internal development before laying, most development takes place in the egg
   (b) **Marsupial**: Birth takes place after limited internal development. Most development occurs after 'foetus' moves to the pouch and attaches to the nipple.
   (c) **Placental**: Long period of internal development, sustained by placenta. Birth takes place at highly developed stage.

Features of the Five Kingdoms (page 267)

1. **Prokaryotae**: Lack nuclei and the organised chromosomes typical of eukaryotes. Some genetic material carried on plasmids. Small (70S) ribosomes but lack membrane-bound organelles. Most have a cell wall containing peptidoglycan (unique to bacteria). Divide by binary fission. Cell wall may be associated with a glycocalyx (capsule or slime layer). As a taxon, the prokaryotes show a large diversity of nutritional modes and lifestyles.

2. **Protoctista**: Unicellular or simple multicellular eukaryotes. A diverse group of organisms, many of which are not related phylogenetically. Includes animal-like organisms such as protozoans and plant-like photosynthetic algae.

3. **Fungi**: Eukaryotic unicellular or multicellular organisms. Heterotrophic and lack chlorophyll. Saprophytes, parasites, or symbionts. Rigid cell walls of chitin. Nutrition is always absorptive. Typical organisational unit in filamentous forms is the hypha. Sexual/asexual reproduction involving spores.

4. **Plantae**: Multicellular eukaryotes, the large majority being photosynthetic autotrophs with chlorophyll. Clearly defined cellulose cell walls. Food stored as starch (and lipid). Primarily sexual reproduction with cycles of alternating haploid and diploid generations.

5. **Animalia**: Heterotrophic, multicellular eukaryotes. Cells lack a cell wall. Blastula stage in development. Further characterisation of animal taxa is based on body symmetry, type of body cavity (coelom), and internal and external morphology.

Features of Microbial Groups (page 268)

1. (a) Wide variety of environments and temperatures; soil, fresh and salt water, on organisms.
   (b) Decomposers and pathogens.

2. (a) Cyanobacteria, e.g. *Anabaena*, *Microcystis.*
   (b) Many examples: *Staphylococcus aureus*, *Clostridium*, *Mycobacterium, Salmonella.*
   (c) Actinobacteria
   (d) *Azotobacter,* rhizobia bacteria, e.g. *Rhizobium*, many cyanobacteria, e.g. *Anabaena.*

3. (a) Marine, freshwater, terrestrial, free-living and as parasites.
   (b) Huge range depending on taxon: pathogens, parasites, phototrophs and heterotrophs.

4. (a) Euglena, diatoms and other algae.
   (b) *Plasmodium* (malaria), *Phytophthora* (blight).
   (c) Foraminifera.

5. (a) Aquatic and terrestrial, including extreme environments.
   (b) Decomposers and pathogens.

6. (a) *Tinea* (athlete's foot), *Candida* (thrush), ringworm, *Pneumocystis.*
   (b) *Ophiostoma* (dutch elm disease), rusts and blights.

Features of Animal Taxa (page 269)

Visible identifying features only including:

1. **Cnidarian features**: Body radially symmetrical. Medusoid (jellyfish) or hydroid (Hydra) body shape. Body wall of two layers separated by jellylike mesoglea. Tentacles with stinging cells for prey capture.

2. **Annelid features**: Body more or less cylindrical and obviously segmented. Move by peristalsis, short appendages, or whole body undulations (leeches).

General arthropod features: Insects, crustaceans, arachnids, and myriopods are all arthropods and share some common features as follows; an exoskeleton of chitin and protein that is shed periodically to allow growth. Paired jointed appendages (legs, mouthparts). Segmented body but with a tendency for loss, fusion or specialisation of segments to various degrees in different groups.

3. **Insect features**: Adult body composed of head, thorax and abdomen. Most adults have one or two pairs of wings (some have secondary loss of the wings). Juvenile forms may be maggot-like or similar to the adult. Three pairs of jointed legs off the thorax. All other appendages (including mouthparts) also paired and jointed. Compound eyes.

4. **Crustacean features**: Most are marine. Exoskeleton often impregnated with mineral salts (calcium carbonate and calcium phosphate). Body covered, at least partly, by a hard carapace. Paired, jointed appendages (often specialised to perform different functions). Two pairs of antennae. Gills often present. Compound or simple eyes. Diverse group; many are highly specialised.

5. **Arachnid features**: Exoskeleton of chitin and protein (as in other arthropods). Body divided into cephalothorax (combined head and thorax) and unsegmented abdomen. No antennae. First two pairs of appendages are feeding structures called chilicerae (fangs) and pedipalps. Terrestrial. Four pairs of walking legs. Many are poisonous with stings or venom sacs. Simple eyes. Spiders produce silk.

6. **Myriopod features**: Terrestrial. Elongated body with many obvious segments bearing paired legs. Head has a pair of antennae and two or three pairs of mouthparts. Centipedes have poison claws behind the mouthparts. Simple eyes. Most millipedes are slow moving, whereas many centipedes are rapid runners.

7. **Mollusc features**: Unsegmented. Muscular foot for movement. Upper body forms a fleshy mantle which may secrete a protective calcium carbonate shell. Scraping feeding organ or radula. Otherwise the group is very diverse. Aquatic and terrestrial. Commonly recognised groups are the shelled gastropod snails and sea slugs and the bivalved molluscs (mussels etc.). The cephalopods (squids and octopus) are highly specialised: the foot is divided into tentacles and they have highly developed eyes.

8. **Echinoderm features**: Marine. Adults radially symmetrical. Body wall rigid (with a skeleton of tiny calcareous plates). Spines are common. Some (sea lilies) are attached, most are mobile. Fluid filled tube feet used for locomotion. In most, mouth points down.

Note: As follows - fish, amphibians, reptiles, birds and mammals are all vertebrates (internal bony skeleton). Paired nostrils and eyes.

9. **Fish features**: Aquatic, ectotherms. Skin slippery with mucus and covered with scales. Gills. Usually well developed fins and tail. Body shape varies depending on swimming mode. Obvious lateral line organ along body. Lack eyelids and tongue.

10. **Amphibian features**: Adaptations for both aquatic and terrestrial life. Ectothermic. Smooth (non-scaly) skin covered with mucous glands. Moveable eyelids. Tympanic membrane for ear present in frogs. Muscular, protusible tongue. Legs and feet (may be webbed) adapted both for swimming and for moving on land.

11. **Reptile features**: Largely terrestrial or semi-aquatic. Dry, thick skin with horny scales or plates. May have legs or be legless (snakes). Tympanic membrane often present. Most lay shelled eggs. Most have well developed eyes.

12. **Bird features**: Endotherms. Horny scales on feet , but feathers over most of the body. Beak, lacking teeth. Adapted for flight (wings, light skeleton) although some are secondarily flightless. Lay heavily shelled eggs.

13. **Mammal features**: Endotherms covered with hair or fur. Glandular skin. Young born live except monotremes which lay eggs. Mammary glands produce milk for young. Teeth often highly specialised. (Internal features: secondary palate and diaphragm.)

Features of Macrofungi and Plants (page 271)

1. **Macrofungi features**: Most are decomposers (saprophytic). Vary from single celled to large multicellular moulds. Rigid cell walls of chitin. Hyphae present in filamentous moulds. Spread by spores. Lichens are a symbiosis between a phototroph (usually an alga) and a fungus.

Note: Mosses, liverworts, ferns, gymnosperms, and angiosperms are all plants and are autotrophic.

2. **Moss and liverwort features**: Lack vascular tissues. Small and restricted to damp environments. Root-like rhizoids anchor plant in ground. In mosses, the plant body is leaf-like. In liverworts it may be leaf-like or a flattened thallus.

3. **Fern features**: True vascular plants. Plant body consists of underground stem or rhizome which bears the leaves (fronds) and roots. Conspicuous spore cases on the undersides of fronds. Clearly defined alternation of generations between large, leafy sporophyte and small, heart-shaped gametophyte.

4. **Gymnosperm features**: True vascular plants. Most are woody plants bearing seeds in cones. Other have naked seeds. Many are evergreen. Male cones shed pollen. Seeds are contained in the female cones.

Note: General angiosperm features: Vascular plants, producing flowers, fruits, and seeds.

5. **Monocot angiosperm features**: Herbaceous (non-woody). Flower parts in multiples of three. Leaves narrow with parallel veins. Seeds have a single cotyledon.

6. **Dicot angiosperm features**: Herbaceous or woody. Flower parts in multiples of four or five. Leaves often broader than in monocots with netted (branching) vein pattern. Seeds have two cotyledons.

The Classification of Life (page 272)

The classification used here recognises five kingdoms: **Prokaryotae** (bacteria, cyanobacteria), **Protoctista** (simple eukaryotes such as protozoans and algae), **Fungi** (mushrooms, moulds, yeasts), **Plantae** (multicellular green plants), and **Animalia** (multicellular animals). Viruses are not included in this classification. Students should classify the organisms provided as follows:

PROKARYOTAE:
Staphylococcus bacteria, *Anabaena* cyanobacterium

PROTOCTISTA:
kelp seaweed, *Amoeba, Paramecium, Euglena*

FUNGI:
mushrooms, *Rhizopus* bread mould

PLANTAE:
Bryophyta: liverwort, moss
Filicinophyta: Boston lace fern
Angiospermophyta: **Monocot**: tulip
Dicot: African violets
Cycadophyta: cycad
Coniferophyta: pine tree

ANIMALIA:
Porifera (sponges): tube sponge
Cnidaria: *Hydra*, marine jellyfish
Platyhelminthes: liver fluke, tapeworm
Annelida: earthworm, polychaete worm
Mollusca: **Gastropoda**: garden snail
Bivalvia: scallop
Cephalopoda: squid
Echinodermata: heart urchin, sea star
Arthropoda: **Crustacea**: *Daphnia*, marine crab
Chilopoda: centipede
Diplopoda: millipede
Arachnida: tarantula, scorpion
Insecta: blowfly, flea, dragonfly
Chordata: **Chondrichthyes**: stingray, shark
Osteichthyes: eel, seahorse
Amphibia: frog
Reptilia:
Squamata: python, lizard
Crocodilia: crocodile
Chelonia: tortoise
Aves: parrot
Mammals:
Prototheria: echidna
Metatheria: kangaroo
Eutheria: manatee, peccary

The New Tree of Life (page 278)

1. The argument for the new classification as three domains is based on the fact that the genetic differences between the Bacteria and the Archaea are at least as great as between the Eukarya and the Bacteria. In other words, the traditional scheme does not accurately reflect the true evolutionary (genetic) relationship between the three groupings.

2. Any one of:
   - Eukaryote groups are given much less prominence, reflecting the true diversity of the prokaryote groups.
   - The Archaea have been separated out as distinct from other bacteria in order to reflect their uniqueness and indicate their true relationship to eukaryotes and to other prokaryotes.

3. The six kingdom classification scheme splits the prokaryotes into the kingdoms Eubacteria and Archaebacteria. These taxa are the same two domains that the three domain classification system uses.

Phylogenetic Systematics (page 279)

1. (a) Morphology recognises the importance of physical features in distinguishing between groups of organisms (it is a simpler and more familiar operation). It also recognises the amount of morphological change that occurs in species after their divergence from a common ancestor.
   (b) Biochemical evidence produces phylogenies that more correctly represent the true evolutionary relationships between groups (taxa).

2. A shared characteristic does not necessarily imply a related characteristic. For example spines on cacti and certain Euphorbia species. A shared derived characteristic is one that is shared between related species and their common ancestor, e.g. hair and its various forms in mammals (horns, quills etc).

3. Parsimony requires that the evolutionary history with the least number of evolutionary events be taken as the most likely (and most likely to be correct) history.

4. Biochemical evidence compares DNA and proteins between species and provides a more direct measure of common inheritance.

5. Data match 5. The mutation from C to T must have occurred separately in pig and whale/hippo ancestors.

6. (a) Pongidae (b) Hominidae

Classification Keys (page 281)

1. The case (presence or absence and features).

2. A *Oxyethira*
   B *Hudsonema*
   C *Olinga*
   D *Aoteapsyche*
   E *Hydrobiosis*
   F *Helicopsyche*
   G *Triplectides*

3. **Insect order (common name)**
   (a) Plecoptera (stoneflies)
   (b) Hemiptera (bugs)
   (c) Coleoptera (beetles)
   (d) Odonata (dragonflies and damselflies)
   (e) Lepidoptera (moths and butterflies)
   (f) Trichoptera (caddisflies)
   (g) Emphemoptera (mayflies)
   (h) Megaloptera (dobsonflies)
   (i) Diptera (true flies)

Keying Out Plant Species (page 283)

1. (a) Silver maple, *Acer saccharinum*
   (b) Japanese maple, *Acer palmatum*
   (c) Red maple, *Acer rubrum*
   (d) Sugar maple, *Acer saccharum*
   (e) Black maple, *Acer nigrum*

2. Any of: Size of the tree or shrub, colour of the bark and flowers, the shape of the winter buds and winged fruit.

3. Before a plant can be classified to species level a number of different features must be considered. One feature is often not sufficient to accurately distinguish

between closely related species within the same genus.

4. The key must be for the genus of plant that the unidentified species belongs to as well as include the species of unidentified plant.

KEY TERMS: Crossword (page 284)

Answers Across
3. Morphology
7. Synapomorphy
9. Plantae
11. Genus
12. Dichotomous
15. Phylum
16. Vertebrate
17. Family
18. Cladogram
20. Archaea
21. Diversity index
22. Distinguishing feature

Answers Down
1. Order
2. Class
4. Fungi
5. Protoctista
7. Kingdom
8. Prokaryotae
10. Arthropod
13. Species
14. Eubacteria
19. Animalia

Variation in Species (page 286)

1. All breeds can interbreed to produce fertile offspring.

2. (a) The grey wolf is a highly variable species in many of its phenotypic characteristics (e.g. size fur thickness, fur colour). There is enough genetic diversity within the species to provide the basis for selection of particular traits. For example, coat colour is highly variable and provided enough diversity to produce the coat colours we see today in domestic dogs.
   (b) Specific desired traits (e.g. short dark coat) are used as criteria to select certain individuals for breeding. Over generations, as some traits are preferentially selected over others, the line begins to breed "true" for those traits and the amount of heterozygosity for the characteristic declines.

Sources of Variation (page 287)

1. Continuous variation is characterised by an exceedingly large number of phenotypic variations (so that a large sample of the population would exhibit a normal distribution for the trait in question). Such traits are determined by a large number of genes and are also frequently influenced by environment, e.g. hand span, weight, skin colour. Discontinuous variation is characterised by a limited number of phenotypic variants. Such traits are determined by a single gene and include features such as chin dimple (present/ absent) and blood groups (A, B, AB, O).

2. (a) Wool production: Continuous
   (b) Hand span: Continuous
   (c) Blood groups: Discontinuous
   (d) Albinism: Discontinuous
   (e) Body weight: Continuous
   (f) Flower colour: Discontinuous

3. Environmental influence expected on: wool production (a), hand span (b), and body weight (e).

4. Student's own plot. Shape of the distribution is dependent on the data collected. The plot should show a **statistically normal distribution** if sample is representative of the population and large enough.
   (a) Continuous distribution, normal distribution, or bell shaped curve are all acceptable answers if the data conform to this pattern.
   (b) Polygenic inheritance: Several (two or more) genes are involved in determining the phenotypic trait. Environment may also have an influence, especially if traits such as weight are chosen.
   NOTE: A large enough sample size (30+) provides sufficient data to indicate the distribution. The larger the sample size, the more closely one would expect the data plot to approximate the normal curve.

5. Many phenotypes are controlled by a combination of genetic and environmental factors. Nutritional influences are responsible for 20-40% of the height variability observed between adults. Childhood malnutrition can result in adults who are below average height (taking into account their ethnicity and gender). Inadequate consumption of protein, calcium, and vitamins A and D have been implicated in this, but other specific nutrient deficiencies (such as iodine) result in specific disorders affecting a range of phenotypes including height.

Adaptations and Fitness (page 289)

1. Adaptive features are genetically determined traits that have a function to the organism in its environment. Physiological 'adaptation' (acclimatisation) refers to the changes made by an organism during its lifetime to environmental conditions (note that some adaptive features do involve changes in physiology).

2. Shorter extremities are associated with colder climates, whereas elongated extremities are associated with warmer climates. The differences are associated with heat conservation (shorter limbs/ears lose less heat to the environment).

3. Large body sizes conserve more heat and have more heat producing mass relative to the surface area over which heat is lost.

4. **Snow bunting** adaptations:
   (a) **Structural**: Large amount of white plumage reduces heat loss, white feathers are hollow and air filled (acting as good insulators).
   (b) **Physiological**: Lay one or two more eggs than (ecologically) equivalent species further south producing larger broods (improving breeding success), rapid moult to winter plumage is suited to the rapid seasonal changes of the Arctic.
   (c) **Behavioural**: Feeding activity continues almost uninterrupted during prolonged daylight hours (allowing large broods to be raised and improving survival and breeding success), migration to overwintering regions during Arctic winter (escapes harsh Arctic winter), will burrow into snow drifts for shelter (withstand short periods of very bad weather), males assist in brood rearing (improved breeding success).

5. Extra detail is (italics) provided as explanation:
   (a) Structural (*larger, stouter body conserves heat*).
   (b) Physiological (*concentrated urine conserves water*).
   (c) Behavioural (*move to favourable sites*).
   (d) Physiological (*higher photosynthetic rates and water conservation*).
   (e) Structural (*reduction in water loss*).

(f) Behavioural and physiological (*hibernation involves both a reduction in metabolic rate and the behaviour necessary to acquire more food before hibernation and to seek out an appropriate site*).
(g) Behavioural (*increase in body temperature*).

The Modern Theory of Evolution (page 291)

Main points are:

Erasmus Darwin (1731 – 1802):
Charles Darwin's grandfather. English physician and scientist who proposed a theory of evolution by the *Inheritance of Acquired Characteristics*. Probably had a great influence on the thinking of Charles Darwin.

John Baptiste de Lamarck (1744 – 1829):
Contributed greatly to the classification of invertebrates. Best known for a mistranslation of his 1809 statement that species had evolved by adapting to a "need". This was translated into English as "desire" and he was ridiculed unjustly by English speaking scientists. (Much quoted example was that he was supposed to have suggested that giraffes could have stretched their necks by *wanting* to).

Thomas Malthus (1766 – 1834):
Wrote an important essay on controls on population growth that helped inspire the evolutionary theories of both Darwin and Wallace. Malthus proposed that the human population would be wiped out unless its birthrate was limited.

Herbert Spencer (1820 – 1903):
Proposed the concept of Survival of the Fittest that he first used in his book *Principles of Biology* (1864). This idea was adopted by Darwin and Wallace.

Charles Lyell (1797 – 1875):
British geologist famous for promoting the work of James Hutton of *Geological Uniformitarianism* (that the same agencies are at work in nature today, operating at the same intensities as they have always done throughout geological time e.g. erosion and sedimentation rates).

Alfred Russel Wallace (1823 – 1913):
Wallace jointly proposed the theory of evolution by natural selection with Darwin. One of the first people to map the distribution of living things leading him to propose the world is divided up into biogeographical zones. He wrote to Darwin of his ideas on evolution by natural selection, spurring Darwin on to publish *The Origin of Species*.

Gregor Mendel (1822 – 1884):
Explained the process of inheritance involving "particles" that are passed on undamaged through the sex cells to the next generation. This was a radical departure from the view of the day that inheritance involved a mere *blending* of parental characteristics.

August Weismann (1834 – 1914):
German biologist who is regarded as the father of modern genetics. He discredited the theory that acquired characteristics could be inherited. He was the first to propose that chromosomes are the basis of heredity.

Theodosius Dobzhansky (1900 – 1975):
A Russian biologist working in the area of population genetics. One of the architects of the Modern Synthetic Theory of evolution. Published *Genetics and the Origins of Species* in 1937; it was a publication that marked the beginning of a new understanding of evolutionary biology. Dobzhansky studied isolating mechanisms and showed how speciation can occur.

Ernst Mayr (1904 – 2005):
A German evolutionary biologist who collaborated with Dobzhansky, Julian Huxley, and George Gaylord Simpson to formulate the modern evolutionary synthesis. Worked on speciation in animals and defined different types of speciation mechanisms. Also proposed in the 1950s that rapid speciation events could occur. This became important for later ideas on punctuated equilibrium.

Julian Huxley (1887 – 1975):
English evolutionary biologist who worked on ritualisation behaviour, neoteny, and allometric growth before collaborating with Dobzhansky, Mayr, and George Gaylord Simpson to formulate the modern evolutionary synthesis. Wrote: Evolution: *The Modern Synthesis* in 1942 after which the new theory was named.

J.B.S. Haldane (1892 – 1964):
English geneticist who contributed to the Modern Synthetic Theory of evolution. An innovative pioneer in population genetics, a field that reshaped modern evolutionary biology.

Sewall Wright (1889 – 1988):
American population theorist and one of the architects of the new evolutionary understanding. Together with Haldane and Fisher, Wright gave evolutionary biology a mathematical basis by working out the mathematical principles of population genetics. This transformed Darwinism into a 20th century science. Best known for his contributions to knowledge of evolution in small populations and the Founder effect (called the Sewall-Wright Effect).

R. A. Fisher (Sir) (1890 – 1962):
English statistician and geneticist who contributed to the Modern Synthetic Theory of evolution. He showed that Mendel's work and Darwin's ideas on natural selection were in agreement, not conflict as some had believed. Made major contributions also to the development of statistical ideas and to knowledge of human inheritance.

Darwin's Theory (page 292)

1. Natural selection can provide the means for species change over time because natural selection will always favour the most adaptive phenotypes (therefore genotypes) at the time. More favourable phenotypes will have greater reproductive success and will become proportionally more abundant in the population. Over time, favourable phenotypes will predominate and the unfavourable phenotypes will become very rare.

Fossil Formation (page 293)

1. (a) Pyritisation: Iron pyrite replaces hard remains of the dead organisms.
   (b) Amber: Conifer resin or gum traps insects or other small invertebrates and then hardens.
   (c) Petrification: Wood is silicified: silica from weathered volcanic ash is incorporated into the decayed wood.
   (d) Phosphatisation: Bones and teeth are preserved in phosphate deposits.
   (e) Tar pit: Organisms fall into a tar pit (mix of sand and tar) and are trapped there. Their remains become embedded in the matrix of sand and tar.
2. Decay.
3. **Transitional fossils** are those processing a mixture of the characteristics of two different, but related,

taxonomic groups. They are important because they indicate that one group may have given rise to the other by evolutionary processes.

The Fossil Record (page 295)

1. (a) Any of: horse, elephant, pig, numerous dinosaur groups, trilobites.
   (b) Any of: tuatara, coelacanth, gingkoes (ancient conifers).
2. Fossilised plants and animals from the fossil record can be compared to living species today thus giving an insight into how they have evolved over time.
3. (a) Layer A (b) Layer H (c) Layer I (d) Layer O
4. (a) Layer E
   (b) It has the same relative position in the sequence of layers and it contains fossils typical of the layer.
5. These rocks may be so old that large organisms with hard body parts were not present to be fossilised (i.e. they may have had soft body parts that decomposed).
6. (a) Layers C and F (b) Layer J
7. Any three of:
   Radiometric dating: Measuring radio-isotope ratios.
   Fossil correlation: Matching up fossil community types with those at another location with a known date.
   Palaeomagnetism: Measuring the magnetic alignment of the rock and correlating this with known magnetic pole directs in the earth's past.
   Fission track analysis: Measuring the number of tracks caused by particles in rock crystals.
8. (a) Layer A: 0 – 80 million years old (< 80 mya)
   (b) Layer C: 80 – 270 million years old
   (c) Layer E: 270 – 375 million years old
   (d) Layer G: Older than 375 million years old
   (e) Layer L: 270 million years old
   (f) Layer O: Older than 375 million years old

Dating a Fossil Site (page 297)

1. **Occupation horizons** (layers in the soil profile with evidence of human occupation) are indicators of human activity some time in the past. Each one is the ancient living floor of the site and can provide information about the type of lifestyle and cultural development of the human occupants.
2. (a) Older than 18 500 but younger than 45 000 years.
   (b) The upper surface is about 18 500 years since it has the hearth (which has been dated) near the top.
3. (a) Pottery bowl: Thermoluminescence.
   (b) Skull: Radiocarbon-14, Uranium-thorium, Electron spin resonance.
   (c) Hearth: Radiocarbon-14, Thermoluminescence.
   (d) Tooth: Electron spin resonance.
4. Palaeoanthropologists document **all** of the remains at a fossil site to maximise the recovery of information. This allows for cross referencing between finds, i.e of hominin and non-hominin species, and gives a more accurate picture of the past environment and ecology.
5. Palaeoanthropology is a multidisciplinary science encompassing palaeontology, geology, prehistoric archaeology, molecular biology, and behavioural science amongst others. Different scientific disciplines provide information on quite different aspects of a site's physical and biological environment and allow any site of hominin activity to be examined in a holistic way. Working in this way, scientists can piece together a more accurate interpretation of past ecology and behaviour.

The Evolution of Horses (page 299)

1. (a) **Teeth**: The equid tooth structure changed from a generalised omnivorous tooth to a more specialised herbivorous tooth able to cope with the tough grasses which became their primary diet. Changes included elongation of the teeth, development of a flat grinding surface, and a hard cement like covering to protect the tooth and cope with the harsh diet.
   (b) **Limb length**: The grasslands were a more open environment which made the equids more susceptible to predation. The increasing limb length enabled the equids to develop a better view of the land around them and thus spot predators, and also to run more quickly.
   (c) **Toe number**: The number toes reduced from four to one and the equids began to stand on tiptoe. These developments promoted an efficient forward and back stride which enabled the equids to become specialised runners (cursors), giving them an advantage in the wide open plains which were developing at the time.
2. The evolution of the modern horse is well documented in the fossil record with numerous fossils, including transitional fossils which show the major features of equid evolution over time (change in body size, limb length, tooth structure, toe reduction). The extensive fossil record has enabled scientists to put together a comprehensive and robust model of horse evolution (including speciation and extinctions).

DNA Homologies (page 300)

1. The similarity of DNA from different species can be established by measuring how closely single strands from each species mesh together. The more similar the DNA, the harder it is to separate them. These studies have confirmed most evolutionary relationships established using anatomical comparisons.
2. (a) Chimpanzee (b) Galago
3. (a) 7 – 8 (b) Approx. 12
4. 45 million years ago.

Protein Homologies (page 301)

1. Chimpanzees and gorillas have virtually identical amino acid sequences to humans for some proteins.
2. (a) They play a crucial role in the respiratory pathway. Most changes are likely to be deleterious so they change very little over time.
   (b) Such proteins are good candidates for use in establishing homologies because the few changes that are retained through time are likely to be meaningful, i.e. represent major divergences in

evolutionary lines.

3. Any of: The rate of change must be calibrated against material evidence for firm conclusions to be made. The functions of the protein may change over time. Clock may run at a different rates in different species.

Homologous Structures (page 303)

1. (b) Human arm: Modified for tree climbing (flexible joints) and improved dexterity of fingers.
   (c) Seal flipper: Modified to increase surface area and streamlined to function as a paddle.
   (d) Dog foot: Modified for swift running in pursuit of prey. Walks on toes, long limbs to provide lengthened, running stride.
   (e) Mole forelimb: Short and strong limb. Shovel-like paw with sharp claws for digging and propelling itself underground.
   (f) Bat wing: Modified into a wing for flying. Very long metacarpals and fingers stretch the skin into a wing.

2. The limbs all share the same basic bone anatomy, although highly modified in some cases. It is possible to match bone for bone, but also recognise how individual bones or bone groups have changed to better perform a new function for the animal.

3. Innate or genetically determined behaviour among animals is inherited in the same way as structural features. While some behaviour is learned, this tends to occur within, rather than between species.

Vestigial Organs (page 304)

1. When an organism adopts a new niche, exploits a new habitat, or takes on 'new' way of doing something, some existing structure may become redundant. Rather than helping the organism to exploit its new way, they may hinder it. Selection pressures may then act against the organs being large. Even if there is no direct selection pressure, the organ may still regress with time as less energy is put into growing a little used body part.

2. The genes that code for it are still present and will continue to express themselves to produce the structure. What is required (for its loss) is an accumulation of mutations that will cause the switching off of the relevant genes altogether.

3. It is possible to see a gradual reduction in the size of the vestigial organ as it progresses from the early ancestor, through **transitional forms**, to modern forms.

Oceanic Island Colonisers (page 305)

1. The plants and animals have arrived on these islands from the nearby mainland communities (South America and Africa). There is no effective way plants and animals could move between these two island groups.

2. Trade winds and ocean currents predominantly move from west to east. This makes traveling from South America to Tristan da Cunha easier than travelling from Africa to Tristan da Cunha.

3. (a) A large island area provides (normally) a greater variety of habitats (and potential niches) for colonisers to exploit, increasing the chances of adaptive radiation and a greater biodiversity.
   (b) The longer an island is isolated from the mainland the greater chance the species there will become unique (either by their own genes changing or the genes of their ancestors on the mainland changing) as there is no exchange of genes between isolated species and their original gene pool.
   (c) Islands that are relatively close to a continental land mass are likely to have a biota that is similar to that of the mainland (because of regular exchanges of genes). The island biota will be unlikely to have the same degree of endemism as an island further from a continental land mass.

4. Features might include:
   - A marine habit: Colonisers must be able to tolerate salt water in order to reach isolated islands.
   - Able to fly but not necessarily strongly: Small birds and insects may be carried on wind currents/blown to an island and then remain there (not strong enough to make a return flight). Stronger fliers, e.g. marine birds, can easily reach offshore islands but are strong fliers and don't remain there.
   - Able to survive long periods without food or water: Isolated island (not surprisingly) are often hundreds to kilometres from land. Travelling to them on rafts of drift wood can take many weeks. Animals with a metabolism that can slow significantly (e.g. reptiles) are more likely to survive the journey.

Natural Selection (page 307)

1. (a) **Directional** selection acts against phenotypes at one extreme of the phenotypic range (such that the phenotypic mean shifts in the other direction) and is associated with gradual environmental change. **Disruptive** selection, in contrast, is associated with fluctuating environments and favours phenotypic variants at each extreme of the phenotypic range, such that intermediate phenotypes are eliminated.
   (b) Directional selection is most often associated with evolution (change in the gene pool over time). Disruptive selection may lead to evolution if one or both of the phenotypic extremes are then subjected to new (different) selection pressures.

2. A shift in environmental conditions can favour one particular phenotype (or phenotypes) at the extreme of the phenotypic range. The phenotypes favoured in the new conditions will have greater reproductive success. Natural selection will act against the reproduction of the unfavourable phenotypes in the new conditions.

3. In a population of variably coloured snails, the environmental conditions could change so that pale forms had thinner shells (for example) and became more susceptible to predation. The darker forms, being better camouflaged, would have better survival and reproduction. Natural selection would favour these darker phenotypes and act against the pale forms, which would have poor survival and reproduction. Over time, the dark forms would predominate and lighter forms would become very rare.

Selection For Human Birth Weight (page 308)

Sample data and graph below. Note: For the construction of weight classes, it is necessary to have a range of weight categories that do not overlap. The data collected should be sorted into weight classes of: 0.0-0.49, 0.50-0.99, 1.0-1.49, 1.5-1.99, etc.

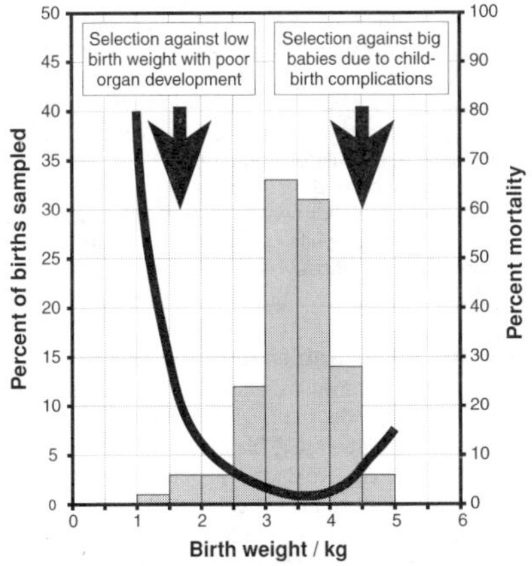

SAMPLE DATA: *Use these data if students are unable to collect from local sources*

3.740	3.830	3.530	3.095	3.630
1.560	3.910	4.180	3.570	2.660
3.150	3.400	3.380	2.660	3.375
3.840	3.630	3.810	2.640	3.955
2.980	3.350	3.780	3.260	4.510
3.800	4.170	4.400	3.770	3.400
3.825	3.130	3.400	3.260	4.100
3.220	3.135	3.090	3.830	3.970
3.840	4.710	4.050	4.560	3.350
3.380	3.690	1.495	3.260	3.430
3.510	3.230	3.570	3.620	3.260
3.315	3.230	3.790	2.620	3.030
3.350	3.970	3.915	2.040	4.050
3.105	3.790	3.060	2.770	3.400
1.950	3.800	2.390	2.860	4.110
1.970	3.800	4.490	2.640	3.550
4.050	4.220	2.860	4.060	3.740
4.082	3.000	3.230	2.800	4.050
4.300	3.030	3.160	3.300	2.350
3.970	2.980	3.550	3.070	2.715

1. Normal distribution (bell-shaped curve), probably with a negative skew (left tail is longer).
2. 3.5 kg (taken from the table: only 2% mortality).
3. Good correlation. Lowest frequencies of surviving birth weights correspond to birth weights of highest mortality.
4. Selection pressures operate at extremes of the range: premature babies have lower survival because their body systems are not fully developed; large babies present problems with delivery as the birth canal can only accommodate babies up to a certain size.
5. Medical intervention has improved the survival rates of very premature babies (as small as 1.5 kg), but this has not historically been the case. Caesarean deliveries have also allowed larger babies to be born. Note that this technology is available to wealthy societies thereby reducing the effect of this selection pressure. Developing countries still experience this selection pressure.

Adaptation and Evolution: Darwin's Finches (page 309)

1. Main factors contributing to adaptive radiation: Absence of competitors on the Galapagos and, partly as a consequence of this, a wide diversity of niches available for exploitation. **Note**: Radiation such as this would also have required a relatively unspecialised founding species with a certain amount of genetic plasticity.
2. (a) If the range of seeds sizes taken by three coexisting species of *Geospiza* are plotted, seed sizes making up the diet overlap in the 2-3 mm range.
   (b) Finches can all feed on small seeds but the upper seed size limit is constrained by bill size. The evolution of different bill sizes has enabled coexisting finch species to specialise in the range of seed sizes they take. When they coexist, finches will preferentially take the largest seed sizes available to them, which is more energy efficient in terms of food handling and enables them to avoid direct competition with other species. In further evidence, on islands where *G. fuliginosa* and *G. fortis* occur alone, both species have bills of an intermediate size. On islands where the two species occur together, they have very different bill sizes.
3. (a) Evidence for **phenotypic plasticity** in Galapagos finches comes from the morphological variability (e.g. in bill size) expressed in a single species depending on whether they exist as an allopatric population or in sympatry with a closely related species. Such plasticity has its origins in the very generalised grassquit ancestor from which all thirteen species derive. Note: DNA analyses have confirmed all thirteen species of birds have evolved from a flock of about thirty birds arriving to the islands a million years ago.
   (b) The original finch ancestor must have been a generalist rather than a specialist, and would have had to adapt to drought, floods, and a volcanic environment in the early years of inhabitance.

What is Speciation? (page 311)

1. Gene flow becomes reduced and the two populations evolve in different directions (until gene flow ceases).
2. Significant geographical barriers would have prevented much gene flow. The large distances between the sparsely populated communities would have made contact a rare event, even for nomadic people. It may have been seen as desirable to introduce 'new blood' into a group when meeting others and women may have been exchanged. More 'hostile gene flow' may have occurred if sexual intercourse was forced upon women during attacks between warring peoples.
3. (a) Geographical barrier in the form of vast oceans.
   (b) Some ducks may still be deterred by mating behaviour that does not match exactly that required by their own species.

Antibiotic Resistance (page 312)

1. (a) Antibiotic resistance arises in a bacterial population as result of mutation. Some bacteria can also acquire these changes in DNA (conferring resistance) by transfer of genes between bacteria by conjugation (horizontal evolution).
   (b) Resistance can become widespread as a result of (1) transfer of genetic material between bacteria (horizontal evolution) or by (2) increasing resistance with each generation a result of natural selection processes (vertical evolution). In the latter case, the antibiotic provides the environment in which selection for resistance can take place. It is exacerbated by overuse and misuse of antibiotics.
2. Widespread antibiotic resistance has implications for the treatment and control of what have been, in the past, quite easily treated diseases. Tuberculosis is one good example. Historically, it was effectively treated with antibiotics, but complacency over its control has lead to increasing multiple drug resistance in the *Mtb* population and a resurgence in the number of TB cases. This has huge implications for public health because more people live with the disease and spread it to more people as a result. In addition, the costs associated with treating TB are now also much higher. Another case is the increasing incidence of hospital-associated infections involving resistant strains of common bacteria such as *S.aureus*. Resistant infections acquired during hospital stays in immune-compromised patients prolong recovery, increase the number of deaths related to incidental infections, and greatly increase the costs of treating patients.
   In general, increasing resistance increases the costs lowers the efficacy of treating disease.

Insecticide Resistance (page 313)

1. (a) Generation times in most pest insects are very short, so successive generations can be exposed (and respond) to the selection pressure of the insecticide in a short space of time.
   (b) Increasingly higher dose rates of insecticide are used to combat increasing resistance (= lack of effective control). This drives the selection process and increases the rate at which resistance spreads in the population.
2. After each insecticide application, only the most resistant individuals remain to reproduce. These offspring are, in turn, exposed to the insecticide. Again, the most resistant survive. With repeated applications of insecticide, the proportion of resistant individuals in the population increases.
3. Resistance to insecticides has implications for how humans effectively control the incidence and spread of vector-borne infectious diseases. Such diseases can potentially be effectively controlled, at low cost, over wide areas by controlling the populations of insect vectors (in the case of malaria, this is various mosquito species). Indiscriminate use of insecticides (e.g. DDT) to control agricultural pests leads to widespread resistance in insect populations generally and reduces (or eliminates) the efficacy of the insecticide in the control of disease. This, in turn, leads to increasing incidence of the vector and the disease, higher disease control costs, and higher costs in treating the disease in infected populations (because incidence is higher).

Chloroquine Resistance in Protozoa (page 314)

1. Chloroquine was very cheap to manufacture, was well tested and safe to administer, and had few side effects. Until resistance developed, it was also very effective at preventing malaria infection.
2. Chloroquine resistance in *P. falciparum* is based on the fact that they accumulate significantly less chloroquine than susceptible parasites. The mechanism for this appears to be due to a mutation at amino acid position 76 conferring an enhanced ability to release the chloroquine from the vesicles in which it normally accumulates in the cell.
3. (a) Combination of drug therapies.
   (b) Temporary withdrawal of chloroquine (for short periods) while using other drugs to retain chloroquine efficacy.

KEY TERMS: Mix and Match (page 315)

Adaptation (O), Behavioural adaptation (U), Chloroquine (Y), Continuous variation (L), Directional selection (A), Discontinuous variation (G), Disruptive selection (K), Drug resistance (D), Evolution (W), Fitness (R), Fossil (J), Genotype (C), Homologous structure (M), Homology (T), Natural selection (S), Pesticide resistance (P), Phenotype (B), Physiological adaptation (E), Population (V), Species (H), Stabilising selection (F), Structural adaptation (X), Transitional fossil (I), Variation (Q), Vestigial organ (N).

Diversity, Stability, and Key Species (page 317)

1. Keystone species are pivotal to some important ecosystem function such as production of biomass or nutrient recycling. Because their role is disproportionately large, their removal has a similarly disproportionate effect on ecosystem function.
2. (a) Grey wolf: Wolves, as a top predator, are an integral component of the ecosystems to which they belong. The wide range of habitats in which they thrive reflects their adaptability as a species. Their diet includes elk, caribou, moose, deer and other large ungulates, as well as smaller prey. Wolves are sensitive to fluctuations in prey abundance, and the balance between wolves and their prey preserves the ecological balance between large herbivores and available forage.
   (b) European beaver: When beavers build dams, innumerable species, many of which may be threatened or endangered, benefit. As well as creating habitat, beaver ponds encourage the growth of aquatic vegetation and also result in increases in invertebrate populations. This in turn provides an enhanced food source for fish, amphibians and birds, which also benefits predators higher up the food chain (e.g. otters and grey herons), which eat the fish. Beavers are entirely herbivorous and their activity is closely tied to the regeneration of deciduous woodland tree species, including aspen, birch, oak, and rowan. Beavers eat the bark of these trees and, by harvesting the trees, promote regeneration and stand replacement.
   (c) Scots pine: The Scots pine has relationships with many organisms. Some are associated directly with the pine itself, particularly epiphytic lichens, mosses,

and mycorrhizal fungi, including the chanterelle and the extremely rare greenfoot tooth fungus. Scots pine provides habitat for a number of plant species with restricted distribution, including blaeberries and cowberries, which play a successional role in the development of the hummocks characteristic of the Scots pinewood ecosystems. A wide variety of invertebrate, mammal, and bird species, some of which are endemic and/or endangered, are also dependent directly or indirectly on the Scots pine (e.g. for habitat or food).

3. The concept of keystone species has a lot of empirical evidence to support it. Keystone species play a disproportionately large role in ecosystem function, so their loss affects the ecosystem in a similarly disproportionate way, and their reintroduction therefore has the potential to restore ecological balance to an impoverished system. There are a number of well known case studies to support this tenet. The key role of beavers (both North American and European) in ecosystems is used to argue for their conservation and reintroduction (e.g. to Britain). Other examples include: Grey wolves in North America: Grey wolves were nearly hunted out of existence in the USA and Europe prior to the twentieth century. Following eradication of wolves in Yellowstone National Park in the early 1900s, elk numbers increased markedly, destroying vegetation and driving beavers and other animals from the damaged habitats. The pivotal role of top predators was determined only after ecological research during the last century and, as a consequence, wolves were reintroduced to Yellowstone and Idaho. The return of the wolves has resulted in a return of biodiversity as the ecological balance has been restored.
Sea otters on the Californian coast: Sea otter populations were decimated as a result of the fur trade from the mid 1700s to 1911. Depletion of the otter populations resulted in a population explosion of sea urchins (on which the otters preyed) and destruction of the local kelp forests on which a large variety of smaller animals depended. As the sea otter populations recover following reintroductions to their natural range, populations of abalone and sea urchins are declining, allowing a recovery of marine plant biomass.

Global Warming (page 319)

1. (a) Carbon dioxide: 37.1% increase
   (b) Methane: 156.6% increase
   (c) Nitrous oxide: 18.7% increase

2. More frequent and prolonged seasonal flooding as well as permanent inundation of land. Increased coastal and inland erosion. Loss of small, low-lying atolls.

3. Increased levels of carbon dioxide, methane, and nitrous oxides act as additional blankets around the Earth, allowing the sun's energy to reach the Earth's surface, but preventing the heat escaping. This means that the Earth slowly heats up. **Note**: The atmospheric concentrations of these gases have increased dramatically above pre-industrial levels since 1750. These levels are considerably higher than at any time during the last 650,000 years (the period for which reliable data has been extracted from ice cores) and are correlated with a rise in global temperature and documented sea level rises. While correlation does not mean cause and effect, the majority of climate scientists accept the theory that the increase in anthropogenic greenhouse gas emissions is causing the rise in the Earth's temperature.

Biodiversity and Global Warming (page 321)

1. Global warming will result in an increased frequency of weather extremes (floods, droughts etc) and a loss of land as coastal areas are inundated. Erosion rates may also increase as a result. Glacial retreats will reduce water supplies and snow lines will increase in altitude. Climate changes may shift the governing physical environment in certain regions (and consequently cause a shift in predominant vegetation). Ocean pH will also fall as a result of CO_2 absorption (again, with consequent changes in biotic communities).

2. (a) In general, crop growing ranges may shrink, expand, or shift. Crop plants may be affected more by higher night temperatures than by higher daytime temperatures. High night temperatures affect the ability of some crop plants such as rice to set seed and fruit. This will cause a reduction in the harvest, and a decrease in the amount of seed available for subsequent plantings.
   (b) Farmers may adjust by planting different crops in some areas, e.g. crops that are able to grow and set seed in the higher temperatures. New strains of crop plants may be able to be developed for the higher temperatures.

3. Evidence suggests that insect populations will be affected by global warming. Butterfly populations in many areas have been recorded as shifting to higher latitudes and altitudes. Fossils of insect browse damage also suggest insect populations will increase in size as temperatures rise.

4. (a) Migratory birds in the northern hemisphere are now not travelling as far south during the winter months (as higher latitudes become more hospitable) and they are making their migrations north up to two weeks earlier than usual.
   (b) Migratory birds may arrive at feeding grounds before the main food supply is ready. Plants with daylength-dependent flowering may not yet be flowering and, as a consequence, insects (and seeds and fruits) may not be in the abundance required to feed the migrants. In addition, the distribution of food resources may remain the same, but the birds are not migrating as far south and may be disconnected from their winter food supplies.

5. As air temperatures rise, so too does the snow line in alpine areas. Animals living on or above the snow line will be forced into smaller areas. If they are unable to move to higher latitudes where the snow line is lower, it is inevitable that they will become extinct in their native ranges as they run out of food and space.

Agriculture and Diversity (page 323)

1. (a) Advantage 1: High yields are maintained by intensive farming even though some areas are retired from production.
   (b) Advantage 2: There is a financial incentive if certain areas are left as conservation estate (income from tourism related to conservation areas and direct

compensation for loss of income from land turned over to conservation).

(c) Intensive farming practices may have a lasting detrimental impact on surrounding conservation estate. The financial rewards of conserving land may not compensate for the income lost through having unproductive land.

2. (a) Habitat loss (hedgerows and woodland areas).
(b) Decline in abundance and diversity of food sources associated with habitat loss.

3. (a)
- Hedgerow legislation to preserve existing hedgerow habitats.
- Policies to preserve or restore woodland cover in previously wooded areas (afforestation).
- Schemes (with financial incentives) to encourage environmentally sensitive farming practices.

(b) Environmental impact assessments and biodiversity estimates would determine the biodiversity levels and the environmental damage in certain habitats (e.g. areas with hedgerows vs areas where they had been removed or had become unkempt). This would identify areas requiring implementation of the biodiversity policies mentioned above, and also provide a baseline to measure the effectiveness of the strategies once implemented.

4. Retaining areas of uncultivated meadow alongside intensively managed pasture is helpful in that it boosts biodiversity in the area and can benefit agriculture in providing habitat for helpful insects, such as predators of pest species and pollinators such as bumblebees. High diversity systems cycle nutrients more efficiently, reducing fertiliser costs, and have better soil structure.

Hedgerows: An Ancient Tradition (page 325)

1. (a)-(c) any advantages of:
- Hedgerows provide habitat and food for wildlife.
- Hedgerows act as corridors along which animals can move between regions of suitable habitat (e.g. for feeding). Corridors are also important for the establishment and expansion of some plant species.
- Hedgerows shelter stock and reduce wind speed, thereby reducing erosion.
- Hedgerows provide habitat for the predators of prey species and pollinating insects. This may benefit the farmer.

2. Hedgerows might be regarded as undesirable because:
- Hedgerows hamper effective use of some farm machinery.
- Hedgerows take up space that could otherwise be used for grazing or crop production.
- Hedgerows provide habitat for competitors to grazing livestock (e.g. hares) and predators (foxes).

3. Retaining well managed hedgerows offers the farmer many benefits. Hedges provide shelter for stock and reduce wind speeds, which stops erosion. Hedges provide habitat for helpful bird and insect species, which can prey on harmful pest insects and prevent spikes in pest populations. The also prevent the spread of wind-borne insect pests. Well managed hedges are also and eco-friendly cost-effective alternative to other types of fencing.

In-situ Conservation (page 326)

1. ***In situ*** conservation uses ecosystem management and legislation to protect species in their natural habitat. By necessity, this involves both restoring the ecosystem and implementing laws to protect the species of interest. Methods include protecting and/or restoring the habitat, and protecting the endangered species from predators, hunting, and illegal trade (e.g. by CITES). Neither tool is effective in isolation; if the species are not protected, there is little point is restoring their habitat and if they are without habitat, there is little point in protecting them.

Ex-situ Conservation (page 327)

1. ***Ex-situ*** conservation methods are often employed when species numbers become critically low or *in-situ* methods are not working. Features of *ex-situ* conservation focus on (1) removal of the endangered species from its natural habitat to a new location, usually a protected or controlled area and (2) captive breeding (or cultivation) involving a managed breeding (seed) register to maximise remaining genetic diversity.

2. Animal species do not all adapt equally well to captivity. Some species will not breed successfully in captivity or have very specific social requirements that might not be met by the conditions. Conversely, those individuals (and species) that adapt most successfully to breeding in captivity are inadvertently selected for survival in zoos, therefore their return to the wild might be compromised.

3. (a) Public education to promote species conservation and increase awareness.
(b) To participate in global breeding programmes to secure the viability of threatened species.
(c) Zoos act as custodians for rare species; they cannot save a species from extinction if breeding is unsuccessful, but they can protect breeding individuals while other plans are implemented.

4. Gene banks and seedbanks provide a store of genetic diversity from wild stocks so that the genetic diversity is preserved in the advent of species loss or decline. Using modern reproductive technologies, gene banks can be used to boost the genetic diversity of inbred populations of endangered species. They also house genetic diversity from which to improve food crops and domestic livestock breeds. Wild species have characteristics (e.g. disease resistance, hardiness) that could be useful in agricultural production and it is important that this store of diversity is not lost.

5. ***In situ*** conservation involves a whole-ecosystem management approach to saving species in their own habitat. Methods include protecting or restoring the habitat, and protecting endangered species from losses (e.g. from introduced predators, illegal trade, and hunting). If whole-ecosystem restoration is successful it offers a good chance of species recovery, even for critically endangered species. It has the advantages of less disturbance to the species involved, it by-passes the need for captive breeding (which is unsuccessful for some species), and it offers a greater chance of long term success because habitat restoration goes hand in hand with species management. ***Ex-situ*** conservation methods are often employed when species numbers become critically low or *in-situ* methods are not working

or are not feasible. *Ex-situ* conservation involves removing the endangered species from its natural habitat to a new location, where it can be monitored and protected more easily. *Ex-situ* methods rarely save species from extinction, and are often costly and labour intensive. Because the breeding stock is also limited, genetic diversity of the species may also become compromised.

National Conservation (page 329)

1. (a) **National Parks**: Areas of substantial size protected and reserved for public enjoyment. Human activity (farming, quarrying etc.) is not excluded but maintained at a level appropriate to maintaining the desirable and characteristic features of the area.
   (b) **NNR**: Smaller and more numerous areas than National Parks, identified under government legislation specifically because of their importance in protecting biological diversity in Britain. In addition to their conservation role, they also function as areas for research and education. They are protected by law but are not guaranteed a protected future (this depends on individual landowners).
   (c) **SSSIs**: Designated by government agencies because of their particular scientific value in terms of their flora, fauna, geologic or physiographic features. Important in protecting natural areas because planning authorities, landowners, or occupiers must be informed of potentially damaging activities within the area. *NOTE: development within these areas does occur however (e.g. for roads or leisure/tourism) and their protection is not complete (esp. as funding for their protection is not assured).*
   (d) **ESAs**: Areas of national significance (determined by the Minister of Agriculture) whose conservation depends on adopting/maintaining/ extending a particular farming practice. Farmers are paid to manage the land in such a way as to conserve the desirable features, e.g. sheep grazing to maintain a chalk grassland, or reducing drainage to maintain water meadows. These managed habitats contain much of Britain's characteristic flora and fauna.
   (e) **The EU Habitats Directive**: A directive for the conservation of natural habitats and wild flora and fauna. Aims to ensure preservation or restoration of biodiversity in the European territory.
   (f) **Natura 2000**: An ecological network of special areas of high conservation value. These areas aim to conserve natural habitats and species of plants and animals that are rare, endangered, or vulnerable in the European Community. Includes Special Areas of Conservation (associated with plants and animals other than birds) and Special Protection Areas (associated with birds).
   Note: Access the web sites pertaining to these organisations from Biozone's **Bio Links** (select sites under **Conservation**).

2. (a) **Conservation of biodiversity**: RSPB, Woodland Trusts and The Wildlife Trusts purchase and manage nature reserves and conservation land for the purposes of maintaining high conservation value habitat (and as a corollary also biodiversity). RSPB is concerned primarily with bird habitat (but this benefits other species also) but has developed wider roles in lobbying for the protection of biodiversity and the promotion of tougher laws for environmental protection. The Woodland Trust is primarily concerned with the conservation of broad leaved woodlands and is also involved in habitat creation. The Wildlife Trusts manage their reserves on sustainable principles with the aim being to enrich wildlife generally.
   (b) **Protection of habitat**: Purchases of land enable land to be set aside for conservation purposes (i.e. not developed for other roles). Careful management helps maintain the integrity and natural features of the conservation estate.
   (c) **Environmental restoration**: The Woodland Trust aims not only to protect existing woodlands but to create new woods through replantings. The aim is to emulate natural processes as far as possible in the types of habitat creation schemes involved.
   (d) **Education and promotion of conservation aims**: NGOs have a vital role in raising public awareness of natural habitats, flora, and fauna, and their value. Education and increased public awareness are the primary ways in which to achieve long term public support for conservation aims. Activities are made known to the public and the public benefits from the activities of the NGOs (e.g. The Woodland Trust maintains facilities to encourage environmentally friendly activity in their reserve areas).

3. (a) The set-aside scheme offers farmers a financial incentive to take at least 20% of their land out of production and leave fields uncultivated.
   (b) Farmers receive compensation for the loss of income resulting from retiring land from production.

NOTES